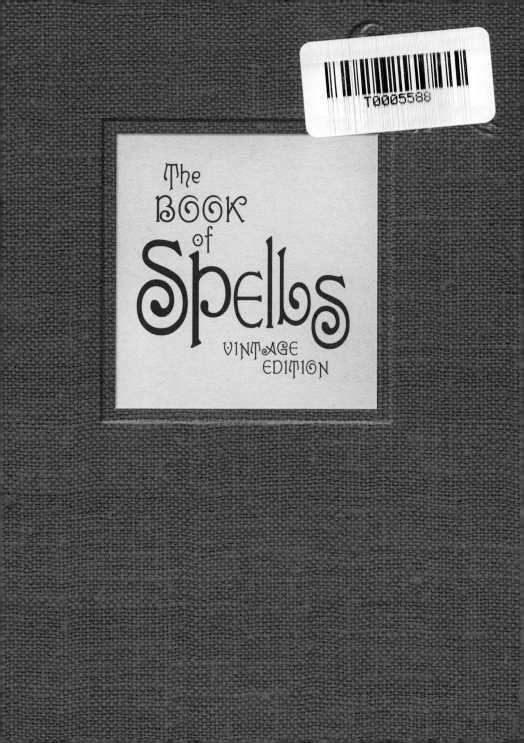

The BOOK of Spells

VINTAGE EDITION

The BOOK of Spells

VINTAGE EDITION

Nicola de Pulford

Bring the power of the good to your life, your love, your work, and your play

A QUARTO BOOK

Published by Sourcebooks
P.O. Box 4410, Naperville, Illinois 60567-4410
(630) 961-3900
sourcebooks.com

ISBN-13: 978-1-7282-9606-7
ISBN-10: 1-7282-9606-4

Library of Congress Control Number: 2009936584

QUA: BSV

Editor & designer: Michelle Pickering
Design assistant: Jessica Wilson
Art director: Caroline Guest
Creative director: Moira Clinch
Publisher: Paul Carslake

Originally published in the United Kingdom in 1998 by Quarto Publishing plc. This edition issued based on the hardcover edition published in 2010 by Quarto Publishing plc.

Printed and bound in China

OGP 10 9 8 7 6 5 4 3 2 1

CONTENTS

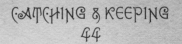

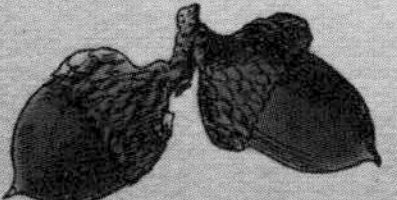

WITHIN OUR INCREASINGLY MATERIALISTIC SOCIETY, MANY OF US HAVE FORGOTTEN THE SIMPLE PLEASURES OF NATURE AND NATURAL MAGIC. IN FACT, IF YOU TELL SOMEONE YOU ARE INTERESTED IN MAGIC, THE STANDARD REACTION WILL BE A RAISED EYEBROW, OR AN AMUSED SMILE. DESPITE THIS SKEPTICISM, AND HUMAN NATURE BEING AS IT IS, THE PERSON WILL, IN THE SAME INSTANT, EXPECT YOU TO PERFORM A SPELL FOR THEM!

Getting Started

Traditional image of a witch

The Occult

An occultist is someone who delves into hidden territory in search of its secrets. Much of the workings of nature are "hidden" to us, and therefore "occult." In the past, occultists—wise women, witches, or wizards, as they have been called—went about their business secretly in order to escape persecution. Fear, greed, envy, and hatred were the root causes of this relentless persecution, which was mainly carried out by ecclesiasts, whose judgment could not be criticized. Witch hunting, and the notorious witch trials, became an industry, bolstering local economies by providing a livelihood for those involved. The Jesuit priest Friedrich von Spee (1591–1635), who dared to speak out against the trials, said: "Often I have thought that the only reason we are not all wizards is due to the fact that we have not all been tortured." This public and manifold slaughter led to a change in the psyche of the populace, and drove any form of magic underground.

NATURAL MAGIC

Until the 17th century, it was an accepted view that nature is alive, and that spirit, mind, and body are linked. In order to heal the physical body, the spirit also had to be in balance. With the coming of the scientific revolution, nature was looked upon as something to be exploited for human gain, with scant regard for the consequences. It is only now that we are beginning to realize that all forms of life have the same nature, and are part of an intricate, living entirety. The components of this cosmos may appear solid and unrelated, but they are comprised of energy, vibrating at different frequencies. We need to develop our ability to recognize the vital energy that flows through nature and animates all life, and to work with the natural magic that is all around us.

Hecate, goddess of magic and witchcraft

A book of spells

REAWAKEN YOUR POWERS

In our modern, subjective world, it is difficult to trust our natural instincts. However, by accepting that spirit, body, and mind are linked, and harnessing the energy of the mind, we can use magic as a way of taking control of our own destinies.

The magic used in this book is a positive force. The spells are all life-affirming, and you do not need to join a coven to use the magical energies of nature. The spells are divided into six sections, the perfect number, and each section contains seven spells, the most magical number, rich with potent symbolism. There are also three spells on sealed pages in the last section of the book, whose power you must only release in cases of emergency, so take care...

THE MAGIC OF THE MIND

Hex symbol for protection

Expensive accessories are not necessary; most ingredients can be found in a local store, garden, or home. The real magic is in your mind and its affinity with the tools you use. Everything in the world is at your disposal, on loan to you from nature, and ultimately to return to nature as you yourself will. Use the spells wisely. They should never be used to gain control over or to harm another living being. If you surround yourself with hateful thoughts, you will attract hatred to you.

Ceres, goddess of growing plants

By performing a spell, you are affirming what you intend to do. Keep it strongly in your mind, and as you begin to feel better about yourself and your situation, the magic will happen. Remember that you are special, and that magic is not rigid; it evolves with you. If you wish to develop your own rituals for gathering ingredients, or make a day trip to secure herbs from a grower, this will add to your concentration for performing a spell, and to your relationship with nature.

MAGICAL INGREDIENTS

Candles are used in many of the spells, as they give a soft, natural light, and help to create the right ambience for focusing your mind. Fire is an important spiritual element. Select a candle of the correct color to aid your magic. Where relevant, colors are suggested for each spell, and there is also a list of magical color associations on page 17. When focusing on a candle, let your mind take in the whole of its golden glow, and as you concentrate,

Candles create a magical ambience

Herbs and oils for magical preparations

visualize the invisible forces all around you and allow your mind to reach a meditative state. It may take some time to learn to focus your mind, but don't give up—practice makes perfect.

Herbs and essential oils are vital ingredients for many spells. Build up a collection of oils to have at hand whenever you need them for your magic, and if possible, buy fresh herbs. You can dry your herbs yourself for those times of year when they are unavailable. If you have the space, grow your own herbs. And remember, the more you nurture them, the stronger your magic will be.

An oil, charcoal, or incense burner, a small flask and goblet, and a sharp pair of scissors are essential items that you will use again and again for performing magic. Make these items special by personalizing them in some way, and use them only for magic. The same applies to any other ingredient or tool you use on a regular basis, or that holds special significance for you.

Essential tools

Phases of the moon

A HELPING HAND

The moon is a powerful aid to your magic, and where relevant, each spell suggests at which phase in the lunar cycle your spell will be strongest. As a general rule, a waxing moon, when the moon is progressing toward its full illumination, will help attract something to you; a waning moon, when the moon's illumination is decreasing after a full moon, will repel; the full moon is the most powerful.

Try to be aware of color, number, and esoteric associations when performing magic, as these are powerful allies and can be incorporated into the spells to tailor them to your needs. Lists of magical associations are given on the following pages.

MAKING YOUR WISH

A pot of gold

Lastly, but most important, magic should be used to elicit your desires gently. At no time should you try to force anyone into a situation in which they would not be happy—the unhappiness will simply rebound back to you. The spells in this book will not lead you to the pot of gold at the end of the rainbow, but if your motives are pure, they will enhance your chances of attracting good fortune. As with most things in life, it is the effort and sincerity you put into your magic that will reap rich dividends.

NUMEROLOGY HAS A PLACE IN MAGIC, AND CAN HELP YOU TO DECIDE WHICH NUMBERS BRING YOU LUCK OR ARE DOMINANT IN YOUR LIFE. IT IS TOO SIMPLISTIC TO DIVINE AN ENTIRE PERSONALITY FROM A NUMBER, BUT THERE MAY BE A NUMBER THAT OCCURS REPEATEDLY IN YOUR LIFE.

MAGIC by NUMBERS

PERSONAL NUMBER

To find your personal number, use the table below to allocate a number to each letter in your name. Add up all the numbers. If the total is over nine, keep adding them up until you have just one digit. For example, "John Smith" is 1+7+5+5+3+4+1+4+5=35; 3+5=8, so eight is John Smith's personal number. If your number adds up to 11 or 22, do not reduce it to one digit; 22 is the "master" number, and 11 represents those who experience revelations.

1	2	3	4	5	6	7	8
A	B	C	D	E	U	O	F
I	K	G	M	H	V	Z	P
Q	R	L	T	N	W		
J		S			X		
Y							

You can use your personal number in your magic in many ways. For example, use it to determine the best day of the month on which to perform a spell, or use your number's color association (listed on page 17) to decide what color clothes to wear on the day of the spell to increase your chances of success. When using numbers in magic, attempt to visualize their attributes and direct them toward your particular need when performing your spell.

1 is the pioneer, the leader, strong-willed and sometimes self-centered. "1" is also associated with material wealth, loneliness, and isolation.	**6** is the perfect number, and represents harmony, beauty, and affection. "6" people are creative and artistic, but they can be fussy and a little conceited.
2 is the number of passive, receptive people, kind and sensitive, but who often get their way by gentle persuasion. It is also linked to psychic powers.	**7** is a magic number, representing the scholar and mystic, the dignified and self-possessed. "7" people may be aloof, as they have difficulty expressing themselves.
3 is a lucky number, representing extrovert, creative, and witty people. They may be extravagant and unable to persevere at one thing for long.	**8** symbolizes intuition, prosperity, and organization. Strong and fertile, "8" people's success is built on hard work, which can make them seem pessimistic.
4 is for loyal, hard-working people who are good organizers. "4" people are guardian angels, fair in all their dealings, and often pay a high price for success.	**9** is for intellectuals and idealists. It is a number of great strength, self-discipline, and ambition. "9" people may seek the limelight and be jealous or fickle.
5 is the number of fast-moving people, curious and impulsive, who hate to be tied down. "5" is also the number of sex and can lead to problematic relationships.	**11** is the number for people who are idealists. "11" people have a strong vocation for their work and often suffer for the sake of others.
22 is the "master" number and incorporates the supreme qualities and attributes of all the other numbers.	

COLORS ARE AN INTRICATE AND IMPORTANT PART OF MANY MAGICAL SYSTEMS. WE ARE SURROUNDED BY COLOR, AND ITS EFFECT IS SOMETIMES BREATHTAKING, LIKE THE SETTING OF A FLAME-RED SUN SPREADING ITS GLITTER OVER A BECALMED SEA. AT OTHER TIMES, COLOR CAN CREATE A SOOTHING ENVIRONMENT; SOFT LIGHTING GIVES A SUBTLE ATMOSPHERE, PERFECT FOR MEDITATION.

the Colors of Magic

HOW TO USE COLOR MAGIC

Every color has its own vibration and unique psychological effect. Color magic has been used in India and China as an intrinsic part of healing work for many thousands of years. Enhance your inner powers and incorporate the strength of colors into your magic by wearing a piece of silk in your favorite color, or a color of appropriate magical significance, close to your skin when performing the spells.

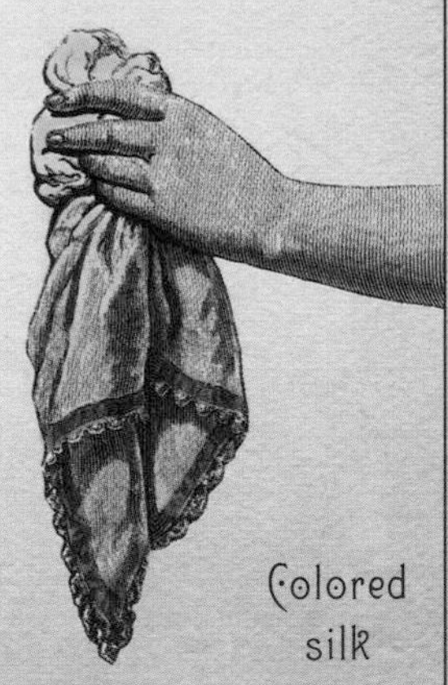

Colored silk

COLORS AND THEIR MAGICAL ASSOCIATIONS

WHITE is for psychic matters, dispelling evil spirits, and for beginning a new phase.	BROWN is a protective shield, and denotes natural wisdom and an affinity with nature.	PURPLE is for spiritual strength, providing a link with higher planes.
RED represents life force, vitality, power, and determination, and attracts good luck.	YELLOW stimulates the mind, and represents achievement and learning.	BLACK is for retribution and communing with the dead, and denotes endings but also the seeds of new beginnings.
PINK is the color of love, reconciliation, friendship, happiness, and harmony.	GREEN is restful and calming, and symbolizes prosperity and fertility.	SILVER is the color of visions and intuition, and brings forth latent potential.
ORANGE symbolizes joy, optimism, and the will to succeed.	BLUE is the color of the spirit, and represents healing, idealism, and occult protection.	GOLD symbolizes great achievement, wealth, and longevity.

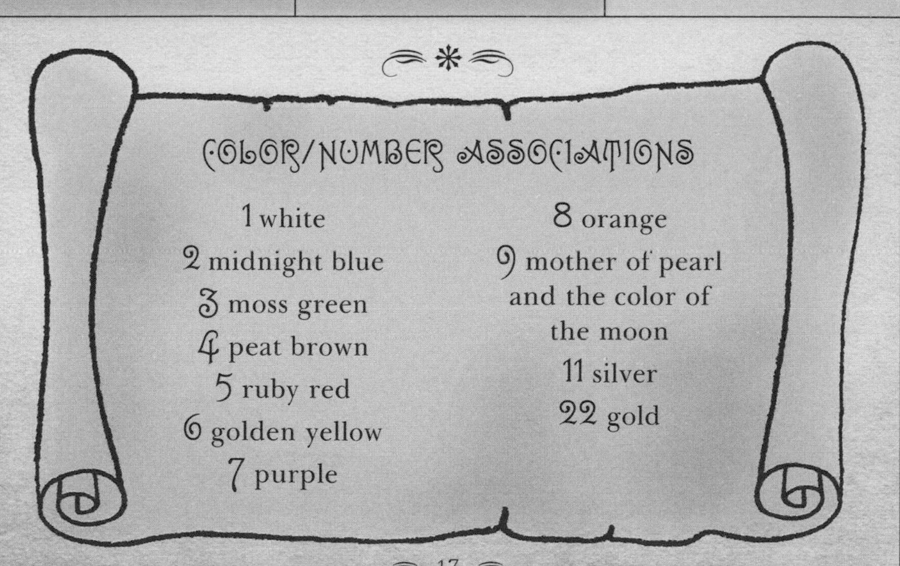

COLOR/NUMBER ASSOCIATIONS
1 white
2 midnight blue
3 moss green
4 peat brown
5 ruby red
6 golden yellow
7 purple
8 orange
9 mother of pearl and the color of the moon
11 silver
22 gold

SACRED TREES FEATURE IN ALL ANCIENT CULTURES. THE TREES VARIED ACCORDING TO GEOGRAPHIC LOCATION, BUT THEIR MAGICAL AND SPIRITUAL SIGNIFICANCE WAS SHARED. THE ACTION OF TOUCHING WOOD, FOR LUCK OR HOPE, STEMS FROM BELIEFS OF COMMUNING WITH TREE SPIRITS.

SACRED TREES & PLANTS

CELTIC TREE CALENDAR

To the Celts, the months of the year were attuned to the lunar cycle. The 13 cycles of the year were measured from full moon to full moon, and they were named after sacred trees. According to the month in which you are performing your spell, you can increase its power by the inclusion of some part of the appropriate tree, as listed in the calendar opposite, either as an extra ingredient or by simply keeping it close by.

CELTIC MONTH	TREE	DATES
Beth	Birch	December 24th–January 20th
Luis	Rowan	January 21st–February 17th
Nuin	Ash	February 18th–March 17th
Fearn	Alder	March 18th–April 14th
Saille	Willow	April 15th–May 12th
Uath	Hawthorn	May 13th–June 9th
Duir	Oak	June 10th–July 7th
Tinne	Holly	July 8th–August 4th
Coll	Hazel	August 5th–September 1st
Muin	Vine	September 2nd–September 29th
Gort	Ivy	September 30th–October 27th
Ngetal	Reed	October 28th–November 24th
Ruis	Elder	November 25th–December 22nd

December 23rd is not ruled by any tree as it is the "day" of the "year and a day." In other words, the four quarter days that make up the extra day in a leap year.

MAGICAL PLANTS AND FLOWERS

From classical times, plants and flowers have been believed to possess supernatural virtues. Flowers have long been used to mark important occasions, from birth to death, and plant extracts form the backbone of much of our modern medicine. Plants traditionally used to accompany divination and visions were mandrake, because its root resembles the figure of a man, and witchhazel, which is still used to

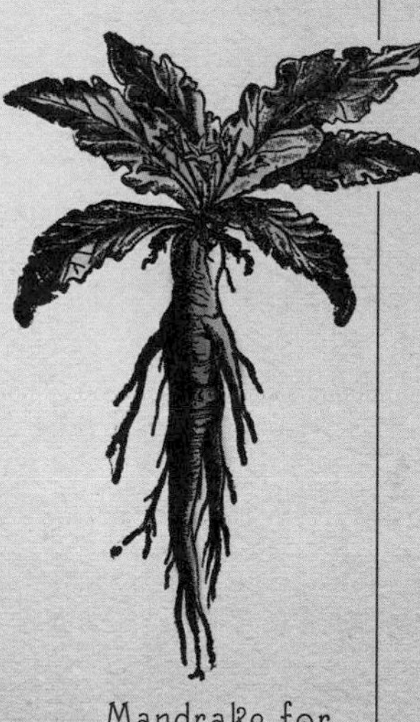

Mandrake for divination

Eyebright
for visions

make divining rods for locating underground water. Eyebright and vervain were among the plants used to aid visions.

Wise women, or witches, of the past usually lived close to nature and cultivated their own special plants. The garden formed a sanctuary, womblike, to nurture the growth of plants for healing and magic. They were used in spells to ward off danger, to attract a lover, and to bring luck, happiness, health, and riches, spiritual or otherwise.

SYMBOLS OF LOVE

Roses are a universal symbol of love, and have been used in love charms for many centuries. They symbolize beauty and perfection, and the white rose is an emblem of silence. Magicians associated the number of petals in a rose to certain meanings; seven signified the seven degrees of absolute perfection, eight petals signified rebirth. Flowers used in love charms often have common names that reflect this, such as love-in-a-mist, forget-me-not, and sorcerer's violet, alias the blue periwinkle. For those forsaken in love, heart's ease, alias the pansy, was a powerful addition to a spell.

Rose and forget-me-not
for love

Lady's mantle and sunflower for luck

ATTRACTING LUCK AND SERENITY

In matters of attracting luck, St. John's wort and lady's mantle were favorites of the medieval alchemists. Other lucky plants include sunflowers, apple blossom, vervain, Solomon's seal, impatiens, and heather. For financial luck, try honesty, a jade plant, hazel catkins, and rosemary. Lilac, honeysuckle, and an almond tree are also said to bring wealth.

For personal protection and warding off evil spirits, oak, rowan, hazel, and hawthorn are traditional favorites. The peony was sacred to the Greeks and Chinese, and in Europe its seeds were threaded onto a piece of white cord and worn around the neck for protection. Betony was preferred by the Italians, who said: "Sell your coat and buy betony."

To create an atmosphere of peace and serenity in your home, the following plants and flowers should not be overlooked: lavender, mignonette, hyssop, iris, chamomile, yerba santa, meadowsweet, hollyhock, holly, and ivy.

Holly for peace

THE WEARING, KEEPING, AND INSCRIBING OF MAGICALLY POTENT OBJECTS THREADS ITS WAY THROUGH ALL CIVILIZATIONS. A TALISMAN HAS THE POWER TO ATTRACT SOME ADVANTAGE TO ITS OWNER, WHEREAS AN AMULET IS PREVENTATIVE, AND WARDS OFF DANGER AND EVIL. PRECIOUS GEMS, METALS, HERBS, AND INSCRIBED PARCHMENT ARE THE MOST COMMON FORMS.

MAGIC SIGNS & SYMBOLS

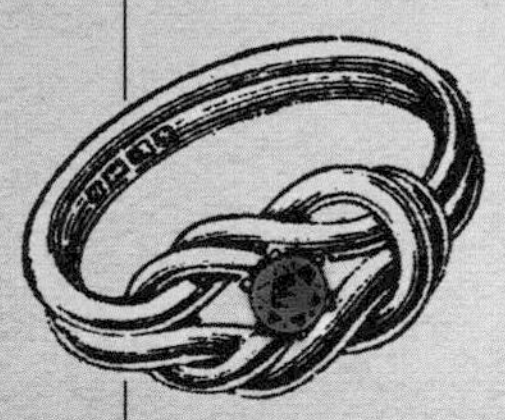

Gemstone wedding ring

MYSTICAL GEMSTONES

Gemstones are especially prized for their natural beauty, financial value, and magical associations. In the past, a magical charm was often in the form of a precious stone, set in a ring or a small filigree cage that was worn on a chain around the neck. The ring is a symbol of attainment, perfection, and immortality, because it has neither a beginning nor an end. It is from this association that the wedding ring evolved, assuming that the wearer had reached a state of harmony and completion. When a precious stone was set in a ring, it was customary for it to be engraved with a magical sign, and for a special herb to be placed under the stone, so that the ring would be imbued with the power of its natural forces.

Incorporate the gemstone associated with the month of your birth into your personal magic charm. For extra luck with your spells, use the stone associated with the month in which you are performing your spell to increase your chances of success.

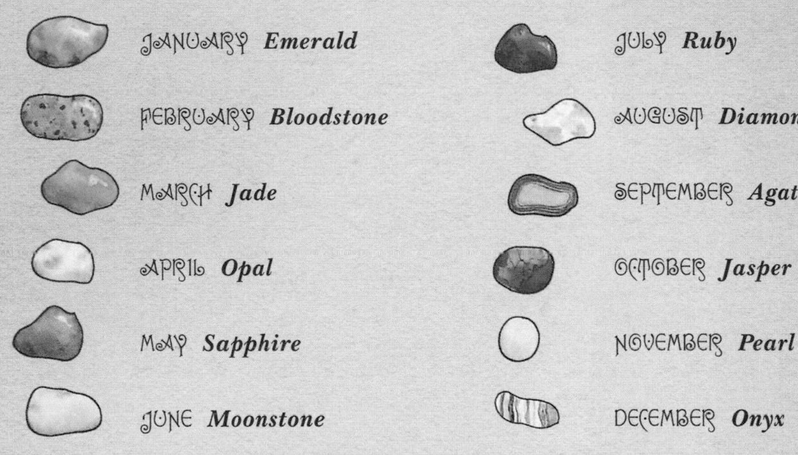

SIGNS AND SIGILS

There are many traditional signs, or sigils, that are honored for their virtues as an integral part of magic. You may wish to use one in your spells, or incorporate it into your special lucky charm.

Amulet against the evil eye

Spring sigil

Look Good, Feel Good

Seven sensuous and spiritual spells, encapsulating the magic of the natural world, to give your body and mind a new outlook. Despite the huge advances in modern scientific medicine, many of us are still drawn to the ancient wisdom of holistic systems of healing and herbal remedies. These spells will increase your physical, mental, and spiritual sense of well-being with the help of Mother Nature.

A Hungarian beauty potion for gleaming hair and youthful zest.

Scented Charm

In the 14th century, a hermit prescribed a beauty potion made from rosemary flowers for Izabella, Queen of Hungary. Izabella, aged 72, was infirm, but after one year of using the hermit's potion, her strength and beauty had recovered to such an extent that the King of Poland expressed a desire to marry her. Rosemary has been used for many hundreds of years and is valued by herbalists as an effective stimulant—"Even to smell the scent of the leaves keeps one youngly," *Banckes Herbal*, 1525.

You will need

Rosemary and sunflower oils

*

Paper and fountain pen with red ink

*

A sprig of rosemary

*

A glass of spring water

METHOD

Dilute 5 drops of rosemary oil into 1 fl. oz. (25 ml) of sunflower oil. Massage the oil into your hair, drawing it right through to the tips. Close your eyes and inhale the wonderful scent. Write your name on the paper with red ink, then dip the sprig of rosemary into the glass of spring water and chant:

"Dew of the sea enhance my charms,
bring love and friendship
into my arms."

Place the paper in the spring water, so that the symbolic essence of you is dispersed, then remove the paper when the ink has faded. Wash the oil out of your hair using the spring water as the final rinse. Wear the sprig of rosemary for the rest of the day to strengthen the magic of your spell.

A Celtic winter spell to revitalize your spirits when days are dark and gloom settles upon you.

the FLOWER of LIGHT

WITH ITS BRIGHT YELLOW FLOWERS, THE CELTIC TRIBES SAW ST. JOHN'S WORT (*HYPERICUM PERFORATUM*) AS A SYMBOL OF THE SUN'S HEALING AND LIFE-GIVING POWER. IT IS A KING AMONG MAGICAL PLANTS, AND PROTECTS AGAINST NEGATIVE INFLUENCES.

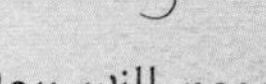

You will need

A large circle of yellow cloth

*

St. John's wort oil

*

2 yellow candles

*

Yellow flowers

METHOD

Spread the cloth on the floor and sprinkle with a few drops of blood-red St. John's wort oil. Anoint the candles with several more drops of oil, and divide the flowers into two bunches. Seat yourself at the center of the circle of cloth and place a bunch of flowers at the edge of the cloth on each side of you. Light the candles and place them at the edge of the cloth, in front of and behind you. Pick two full, perfect blooms, and hold one in the upright palm of each hand. Focus your mind on the glow of the candle in front of you and chant:

"Oh healing light,
surround me now,
relieve my spirit's
darkest hour."

Imagine the scented light being drawn from the candles into the flowers on your palms, and from there feel it permeating the whole of your body. Try to keep your concentration for about 20 minutes; when you rise the melancholy will fall from you. To complete the spell, take the two flowers in your hands and give them back to Mother Earth.

If you are not performing at your peak, peppermint, the flower of refreshment, will lift your spirits.

Peppermint Cream

Peppermint (*Mentha piperita*) was revered by the ancient Egyptians, Greeks, Chinese, Japanese, and Romans. Greek athletes used peppermint oil as a muscle toner before competitions and more generally as a refreshing perfume. The name comes from the Latin *mente*, meaning "thought," and the Romans used it to stimulate the brain. You need to set aside half an hour at any time of the day or night for this ritual remedy.

You will need

Peppermint tea

Peppermint oil

A large bowl of water

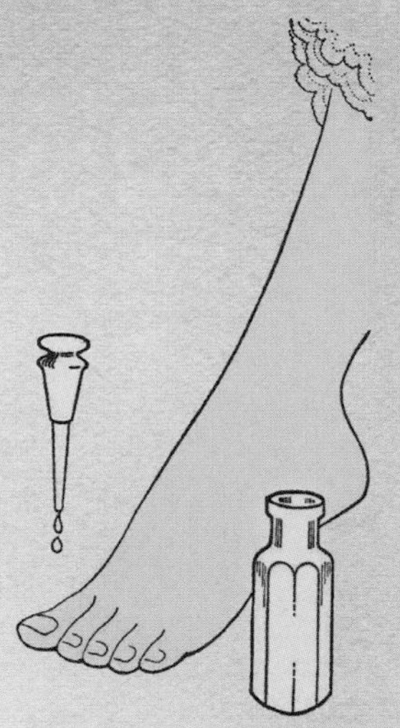

METHOD

Brew the peppermint tea and leave it to steep for 5–10 minutes. Meanwhile, prepare a foot bath by adding 5 drops of peppermint oil to a large bowl of fairly hot water. Do this in a methodical manner, thinking only of the task at hand. Stir the peppermint oil into the water in a clockwise direction, and while you are watching the circles of oil disperse, chant:

"Dispel the cloud upon my brow, uplift my spirits here and now."

Sit in a comfortable chair that hugs your body, and sip the tea as you soak your feet. Close your eyes and feel the warmth spreading up your body from your feet and meeting the hot peppermint tea you are drinking. As the warmth and essence engulf your senses, your whole body will glow, revitalized.

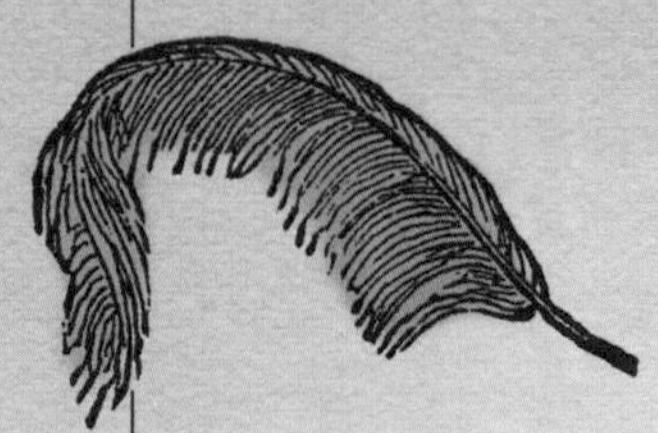

A Native American ritual to put your body, mind, and spirit in harmony.

Walking the Good Red Road

According to Native American beliefs, we are spiritual beings on a human journey, part of the One Great Spirit. Our bodies are shells that will, like all living things, return to Mother Earth when we die, but our spirits will return to the whole spirit, the unseen world. Many of us live in cities with little contact with Mother Earth; we no longer walk with nature, in the embracing Circle of Life. This ritual will help to restore your spiritual balance. The colors red, black, yellow, and white represent the races of humanity and the four quarters of the Circle of Life.

You will need

A feather

*

A long piece of red ribbon

*

Red, black, yellow, and white beans

METHOD

Find a place where you can be alone with the natural world. Imagine you are walking through a door, leaving your everyday world behind you. Walk in a clockwise direction until you feel a desire to stop; place your feather on this spot. Continue to walk; if this spot calls to you again, this is "your place." If it doesn't, repeat this process until you find "your place."

*

Arrange the ribbon in a circle with the feather at its center. Place some colored beans in each quarter of the circle. Pick up the feather and sit in its place. Look around you and drink in the spirit of the place. Open all your senses and breathe the air common to all living beings; like a web, it connects you to them. Feel the breeze on your face, the feather in your hand, and become in balance. Keep the beans and feather safely, as a reminder to perform this ritual as often as possible.

THE MAGIC OF ANCIENT CIVILIZATIONS PROVIDES A FASCINATING INSIGHT INTO TODAY'S MAGIC. WRITINGS AND ARTIFACTS FROM THE ANCIENT WORLD OF THE EGYPTIANS, BABYLONIANS, AND GREEKS ALL ALLOW INTRIGUING GLIMPSES INTO THE MAGIC OF THE PAST AND HOW IT HAS INFLUENCED PRESENT-DAY PRACTICES.

Hieroglyphics

ANCIENT MAGIC

Isis

EGYPT

The Egyptians were the master magicians in the ancient word. It was said that "Ten measures of magic were given to the world. Egypt took nine, the rest took one." Egyptian magic developed into a complex web of beliefs in reincarnation and the ability to see divinity in all things, both the living and the inanimate. They were the first to categorize magic into types: *ua* or "low magic" was magic for the physical world of health, money, and luck; *hekau* or "high magic" was associated with the spirit.

Osiris

Egyptian magic comes to us largely through "The Book of the Dead," a source book of spells, rituals, and incantations to ward off danger and evil in the soul's long journey into the afterlife.

To the Egyptians, words were magical, and in order to preserve them, hieroglyphics were created. One of these hieroglyphics, the Eye of Horus, is often used in magic. Horus was the son of the two chief deities, Osiris and Isis. Osiris's brother Seth killed Osiris out of jealously. Horus avenged his father by attacking Seth, but during the battle Seth gouged out Horus's eye. The eye was considered a symbol of the soul in ancient Egypt, so without it, Horus would be denied entry to the afterlife. Thoth, the bird-headed god of reckoning, returned the eye to Horus in the form of an amulet. To guarantee entry into the underworld, ancient Egyptians used to place precious amulets featuring the eye on their dead.

Haitian, Wiccan, Voodoo, Obeah, and Indian mystical traditions inherit the symbolism of the eye as the "all-seeing eye" or the "third eye."

Eye of Horus

Horus

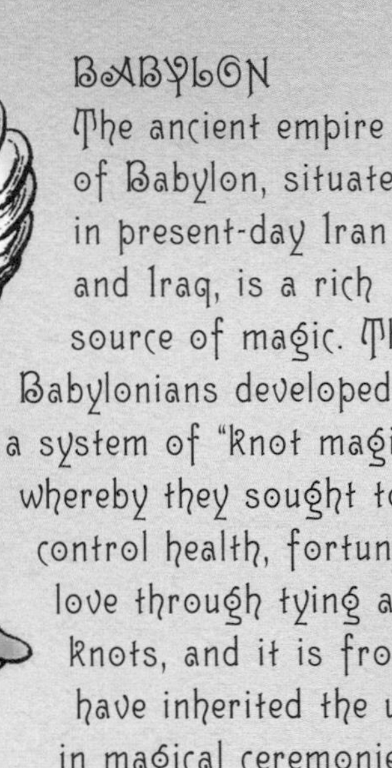

BABYLON

The ancient empire of Babylon, situated in present-day Iran and Iraq, is a rich source of magic. The Babylonians developed a system of "knot magic," whereby they sought to control health, fortune, and love through tying and untying knots, and it is from Babylon that we have inherited the use of wax figures in magical ceremonies. A key figure in the Babylonian magical system is Ishtar, the goddess of fertility and love, who was invoked to exorcise evil spirits. The eight-rayed Star of Ishtar was used as a protective talisman. Ishtar is the forerunner of the genie, a figure conjured up from smoke and incense to grant your every desire.

Star of Ishtar

Ishtar

❋

GREECE

Today, we consider the ancient Greeks to have been logical and scientific, yet in reality, the magical beliefs of old were merely cloaked in reason by the philosophers. Pythagoreans were renowned as mathematicians, but they also practiced magic, though infused with philosophical speculation.

Pythagoras

A significant aspect of Greek magic was the sacred "Qualities of Names," the belief that the life of a person is invested in his or her name. Names, alphabets, and letters were invested with great magical powers; the word "abracadabra" is of Greek origin. Originally the letters were written in the shape of an inverted pyramid and worn around the neck as a charm against evil. The letters were also used to ward off illness. Inscribed onto papyrus, they were thrown into an eastward-running stream, so that the disease as well as the letters were carried out to sea and erased. Ancient Greeks often would not reveal their names to casual acquaintances, so that harmful spells could not be carried out against them. Likewise, in military campaigns, the names of battles or of generals could not be uttered in case they were overheard by the enemy and used to win advantage.

ABRACADABRA
ABRACADABR
ABRACADAB
ABRACADA
ABRACAD
ABRACA
ABRAC
ABRA
ABR
AB
A

Abracadabra charm

Greek talisman

The Greeks also carried out sacrifices. When a new building was being erected, a cock, ram, or lamb would be killed and its blood let on the foundation stone, after which the animal would be buried beneath the stone.

Sacrificial ram

A spell based on ancient Druidic beliefs to lift your spirits.

Regenerating Massage

Vervain (*Verbena officinalis*) was one of the Druids' most sacred herbs, and was used to cleanse their altars, for divination, as amulets, and for their most important spells. It was also mentioned in witch trials, where it was thought to make the wearer invisible and able to fly. This spell will not enable you to fly, but can certainly raise your spirits.

You will need

Dried or fresh vervain leaves

*

Rose otto, sandalwood, and sunflower oils

*

2 blue candles

METHOD

Gather or buy your vervain leaves on the day of the full moon, then charge them with the moon's rays by facing the moon, holding the leaves in your outstretched hands, and repeating:

"Imbue my sacred herb with light, with power full both day and night."

Now that the vervain is charged, you may keep it to use whenever you wish. Before the massage, put the vervain leaves in boiling water and leave to infuse for 10 minutes. Meanwhile, dilute 2 drops of rose otto oil and 5 drops of sandalwood oil into 1 fl. oz. (25 ml) of sunflower oil. Next, strain the infusion, add it to your bathwater, and soak for at least 10 minutes to gain its full effect. In a warm room lit with the blue candles, massage yourself with the oil. Start with your legs, stroking from ankle to thigh, and travel up your body. Finish by covering your eyes with your hands and breathing deeply for a few seconds.

A summer celebration carried out from the Andes to the Himalayas for physical well-being.

Solar Power

This is a seven-day spell best performed at the time of the summer solstice, June 21st. June is the time of the "strawberry moon," when European farmers used to gather their strawberries and other crops by the light of the moon. It is "the door to the year," the time of maximum light and minimum darkness, when the door symbolically opens to let the life-giving sunshine and all things good in, and exclude evil spirits. Prepare the spell a few days before this date, as you need to check that the mirrors are positioned correctly.

METHOD

Choose a room in your home that catches the early morning sun, as you need to bathe yourself in solar light. Place each mirror behind a vase of flowers on opposite sides of the room, so that one of the mirrors will catch the sun's rays and reflect them onto the other mirror. Mark the candles into seven equal segments, and place them near the mirrors. As soon as the sun comes to your mirrors, light the candles. While the candles burn to the first mark, wrap the end of the ribbon around your right index finger and allow the rest to trail. Stand centrally between the mirrors, in the beam of light, and slowly turn clockwise, gathering the sun's rays to your body with the trailing ribbon and focusing the ray with your mind. Ask the sun for health and spiritual well-being and thank her for being with you. Repeat for the next six mornings, burning one segment of the candles on each morning of the spell.

You will need

2 mirrors

*

2 vases of orange flowers

*

2 orange candles

*

A length of white ribbon

A dance in the dew, from European folklore, to give you an early morning pick-me-up.

Dawn Delight

From classical mythology to country lore, the dew has always had magical significance as a beauty enhancer and giver of strength. Medieval alchemists collected dew for their potions and called it "water from heaven." Ladies and country girls alike would go to the fields to "meet the dew" and wash their faces with it. Perform this spell at dawn, whenever the weather is warm enough.

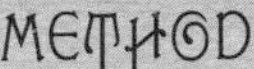

You will need

A flower blossom

*

A light, flowing robe

*

A pair of sandals

METHOD

A meadow is the ideal place to perform this spell, but a garden lawn will suffice. Buy or pick a flower blossom the day before the spell, and keep it safe. Rise early the following morning, and dress in a robe and sandals. Holding the flower, go to your meadow in silence, inhaling deeply the sweet scent of morning. Remove your sandals and savor the velvety touch between your toes. Wash your face and hands in the dew, invoking:

"Embrace me from the break of day to the setting of the sun; I thank you air, fire, water, earth, blessed be the one."

*

If the inclination takes you, remove your robe and let the magic of the dew enfold the whole of your body.

Catching & Keeping

Seven spells for attracting and keeping a lover. If you wish to attract a new love, or tip the balance with someone you have been attracted to for some time, these spells are for you. But beware; this magic will not help if the person you have in mind is already in a loving relationship, or is unsuited to you. If you already have a partner and wish to spice things up, or encourage constancy, a little loving magic may be just what you need.

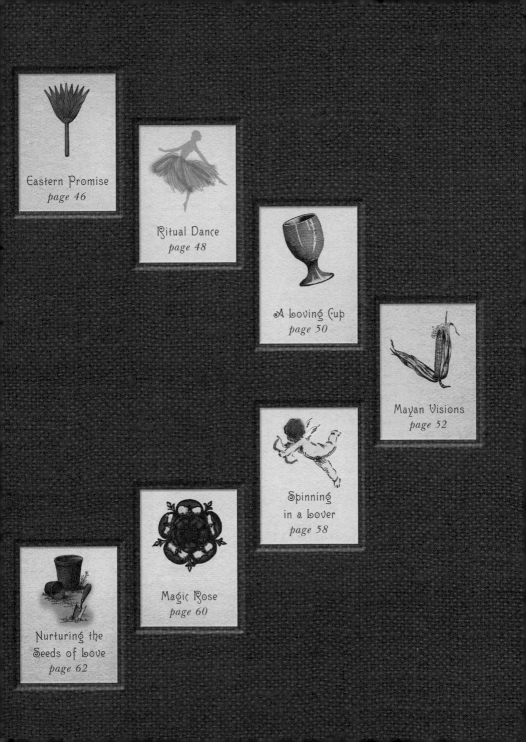

A sensual ritual from India to enhance the libido.

Eastern Promise

You will need

"The Spices of Life"

*****

An oil burner

*****

Musk and patchouli oils

*****

Pink candles and some wine

PREPARE "THE SPICES OF LIFE" RECIPE THE DAY BEFORE YOU WISH TO USE IT, AND PUT ALL YOUR LOVE INTO IT AS YOU WORK.

The Spices of Life

Put the oil in a heavy pan, heat, and throw in cloves, cinnamon, and cardamom. After 2 minutes add chopped onions and cook on medium heat for 5 minutes. Mix all the other spices together and add to the onions. Cook slowly for 10 minutes, stirring occasionally. Add the meat, fish, or vegetables, stir well to coat with the spices, then add the garlic. Add enough water to cover the ingredients. For meat, simmer for 1½ hours; for fish or vegetables, simmer for ½ hour. When cool, place in a refrigerator till required.

Ingredients

- *4 tbsp oil*
- *3 whole cloves*
- *small piece of cinnamon bark*
- *1 green cardamom pod*
- *3 large onions*
- *1 tsp each of ground cumin, coriander, ginger, turmeric, and salt*
- *¼–1 tsp chili powder, according to taste*
- *1 lb. 6 oz. (600 g) meat, fish, or vegetables*
- *2 tsp mashed fresh garlic*
- *basmati rice*

METHOD

Create a sensual ambience by vaporizing a few drops of the essential oils in the oil burner, and lighting the candles. Cook the rice and heat the main course. As you stir it, chant:

"Aum mani padme hum."
(Hail to the jewel in the lotus.)

With your partner, partake of the wine and food. Afterward, you will be in harmony with each other, and ready for anything!

An African dance ritual to seal your relationship.

RITUAL DANCE

THE ANCIENT RITES THAT MARK THE PASSAGE FROM ONE STAGE OF EXISTENCE TO ANOTHER OFTEN INCLUDE DANCE RITUALS. THROUGHOUT AFRICA, DANCE RITUALS ARE PERFORMED FOLLOWING A BIRTH, THE NAMING OF A CHILD, AND AT ALL OTHER GREAT OCCASIONS. FOR MAXIMUM EFFECT, THIS DANCE SHOULD BE PERFORMED IN THE OPEN AIR WITH A FULL MOON. IF THIS IS IMPRACTICAL, A SMALL OIL BURNER CAN BE USED INSIDE YOUR HOME INSTEAD OF A FIRE.

You will need

Wood to make a small fire

*

A flask of wine

*

13 small pebbles

*

A green-leafed branch

METHOD

Go with your partner to a quiet spot where you can safely light a small fire; this is the center of your magic circle. Take a drink of wine from the flask, which should only be used for magical purposes. Make a spacious circle with the pebbles and stay within that circle. Start by looking deeply into the fire, and when you both feel its spirit enter you, dance clockwise seven times around it. At the end, pluck a leaf from the branch, both of you moisten it with wine, then burn it on the fire, saying:

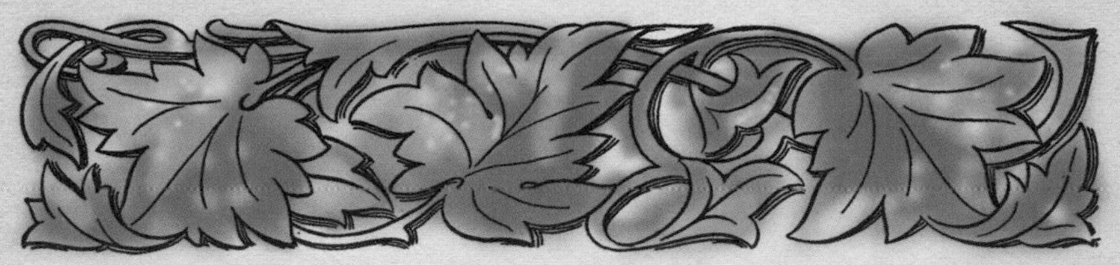

"This we have both shared,
with fire, water, air, and earth;
our hearts will now stand firm,
and the seed of love will grow."

Drink a toast and extinguish the fire with the remaining wine.

An Italian potion of liqueur and herbs, believed to have aphrodisiac qualities.

A Loving Cup

Many expensive foods and drinks are said to act as aphrodisiacs, but the only proven one is alcohol. *Strega* is the Italian word for "witch." The liqueur called strega comes from the Benevento region of Italy, well known for witchcraft. Strega was said to have been brewed originally as a witch's potion. In England, mead, which is made from honey, was considered to be an aphrodisiac. It was drunk for one month after a wedding, to make the couple sexually potent. This is the origin of the word "honeymoon." Liqueurs and wines are the best stimulants, but should only be taken in small quantities, with a little magic thrown in for special effect. In Italy, basil was worn by courting couples as an emblem of love.

METHOD

Keep your silver coin close to you until there is a full moon, then hold it in the palm of your hand under the moonlight, focusing your mind on your lover, to charge the coin with the moon's power. When you have done so, and on the night you wish to use the "Loving Cup," pass the charged silver coin over enough basil and sage leaves to line the bottom of the goblets. This will transfer the moon's power to your love potion. Line the goblets with the charged leaves and pour in the liqueur; leave for one hour before partaking with your partner. The mood for love will enter you both quite quickly.

You will need

A silver coin

*

Some basil and sage leaves

*

2 goblets

*

A little strega or mead liqueur

A spell based on ancient Mayan traditions to help you see your future love.

Mayan Visions

The Maya communicated between this world and the "other world" with words. All spirits speak, whatever their material appearance, and words are the essential thread that link us to those spiritual forces. Focusing on an obsidian stone, the "stone of light," will help you to communicate with this spirit world and see a future lover. Such visions require great concentration and diligence, and should be accompanied with offerings of maize gruel, the basic food of life and a primeval sacred liquid.

METHOD

Make some maize gruel by mixing a little maize flour and spring water, and heating gently until the mixture thickens. When the gruel has cooled, purify the obsidian stone by coating it with some gruel. It is important that you do this with your hands and no other medium. Place the obsidian stone in the bowl, and fill to just above the stone with spring water. Rinse your hands in some spring water to remove the remaining gruel. Light the blue candles and place them on one side of the bowl. Seat yourself on the other side, facing the bowl and candles. Concentrate first on the candles, speaking your wishes in a soft, singsong voice. Continue speaking and transfer your gaze to the obsidian. Look deeply into the stone and focus on your words becoming part of it. You may have to repeat this spell several times before you are ready to "see."

You will need

Some maize flour and spring water

*

An obsidian stone

*

A small bowl

*

3 blue candles

THE MAGIC OF THE AMERICAS IS AS VAST AND VARIED AS THE CONTINENT IT SPANS. MANY RELICS OF THIS CONTINENT'S MAGICAL AND RITUAL PAST HAVE SURVIVED, AND SOME TRADITIONS ARE STILL PRACTICED BY NATIVE PEOPLES.

MAGIC of the AMERICAS

NATIVE AMERICAN

The sacred circle or hoop was central to all Native American life and magic. A circle represented the belief that life was a complex web where everything and everyone is connected. With its center equidistant from any point on the circumference, the circle reflected the belief that all life force, man or mineral, was equal. If one part of the circle was damaged, this would in time be detrimental to the other parts, as we all share one Mother Earth.

Sacred circle

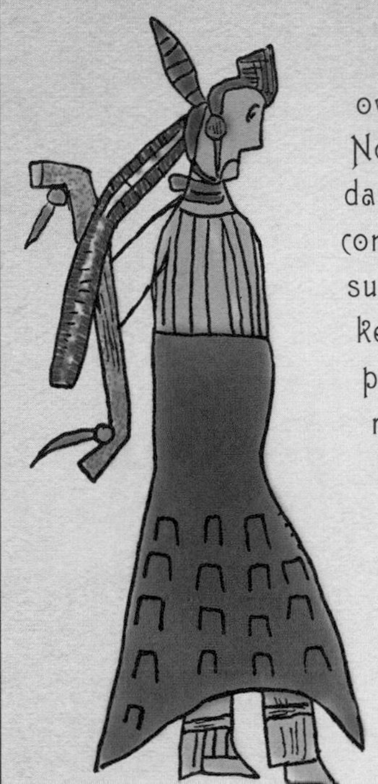

Medicine bag worn across the shoulder

The medicine wheel was used in over 500 different systems of belief in North America, and some existing wheels date back over 1,000 years. They were constructed from stones and aligned to the summer solstice. Medicine bundles were also kept, and their contents, such as feathers, pebbles, seeds, wood, and animal claws, represented allies in the natural world. The bundles were used for protection, seeking visions, and sun dances, and the contents were sacred.

Feathers were worn as they were believed to possess spiritual qualities, which were embodied by the bird from which the feathers came. The eagle was regarded as the most spiritual of birds, with the best vision and the ability to fly to great heights, carrying the prayers of the people to the "great spirit." Its feathers were used to decorate shields and fetishes. Ritual rattles were used to scare away evil spirits. Native American rituals and magic were designed to bring its people into harmony with themselves and as part of the Circle of Life.

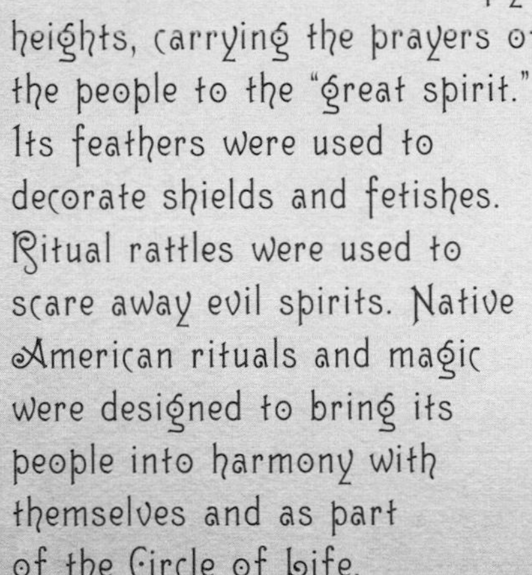

Hopi eagle

Itzamna

MAYAN

To capture the wisdom of the universe, the Mayans built vast and beautiful temples at the top of pyramids. Ball courts were erected close to the temples, and a ritual game, which included sacrifices, was played there to appease the life-giving powers. Mayan magic was based around the growing of maize. A special gruel of maize and water was offered to the maize god, Ah Mun, and other deities in elaborately painted vessels; the gruel represented life and rebirth. Itzamna was the chief god of the Mayans; he was benevolent, and bestowed the gifts of drawing and writing, and arranging land holdings.

The Mayans believed they had two souls, one of which was invisible and divided into thirteen parts. These parts could be stolen by evil witches and sold to the earth lord, Ah Puch. Shaman seers would try to find the missing piece with the aid of "talking stones," which were used to focus spiritual forces and for visionary journeys. "Talking stones," or "stones of light," are one precursor of the crystal ball.

Ah Puch

INUIT

The magical world of the Inuit, or Eskimo, contained a celestial world above and an underworld below, dominated by the goddess Sedna. Sedna's father had found his daughter so unruly that he took her far out to sea in a boat, to cast her overboard. Sedna held tightly to the side of the boat, but her father chopped off her fingers, which turned into seals when they touched the water. The sea is the most important source of food to the Inuit, and shamans and other members of the group performed masked rituals to ensure its continued bounty, invoking the help of the moon spirit, the mighty hunter.

In legend, the goddess Sedna's fingers turned into seals

Ritual mask

Belts made of bird skulls and talons were worn for protection while hunting on land. The spirits of animals were charmed, so they could only be killed out of necessity. Thanks were given to appease the spirits, and any unused parts of the animal had to be returned to the place where it had been trapped, so that its spirit could be reborn.

Moon spirit

An old English spell to attract a special lover.

Spinning in a Lover

Traditionally, the wood of the spindle (*Euonymus europaeus*) was used to spin wool, mostly by unmarried girls known as "spinsters." A round stone with a whole in the middle was fitted over the end of the spindle to keep it turning, and so grew its association with the male and female. If you cannot obtain spindle, willow will work just as well, or buy a ready-made spindle. To attract a special lover, carry out this spell on a Friday, the day sacred to Venus, goddess of love, and on a waxing moon for maximum power.

METHOD

To attract your ideal partner, start this spell on a moonlit Friday evening. Picture his or her physical and spiritual being in your mind's eye, and attach a magical name to him or her. Inscribe this name on the side of the candle using the toothpick. On a narrow strip of paper, write your name down, then braid the ribbons around the paper, keeping your ideal partner in your mind's eye all the while. Take the braided ribbons, candle, and spindle to the moonlight, asking Venus to bless them. Set the candle down and light it. Concentrate on its glow and picture yourself hand in hand with your new love. Wind the braided ribbons around the spindle in a clockwise direction as you watch the candle melt your lover's name. Seal each end of the ribbon to the spindle with melted wax. Keep the spindle close to you when you go to bed. Unbraid the ribbons the following day to free the spell and bring love to your side.

You will need

A pink candle and toothpick

*

A strip of paper

*

Red, green, and white ribbons

*

A length of spindle wood

An old Germanic spell to attract the man or woman of your dreams.

Magic Rose

This spell originates from old Germany, where roses were emblems of silence. A white rose, or sometimes simply a symbol of a white rose, was worn by those wishing to speak secretly to each other. In Germany and other parts of the Low Countries, a rose was often sculpted or painted over the banqueting tables; words spoken beneath it were not to be revealed. Amorous chatter, in particular, would remain secret as the rose was sacred to Venus, the goddess of love, who is said to have blushed when Jupiter caught sight of her bathing, turning a white rose to red. Perform this spell in June at the time of a waxing moon.

METHOD

Obtain a red and a white rose; they should not be fully open. Older varieties with a luscious scent are preferable, such as "Mme Hardy" or "Boule de Neige" white roses, and "Souvenir de Docteur Jamain" or "Cardinal de Richelieu" red roses. On the scroll of paper, write a description of the ideal lover you would like to attract. Wrap the scroll around the lock of your hair. Take the two roses and cut them both in half. Place a white half to a red half, enclosing both the scroll and the lock of your hair between them. Bind the two halves together with the pink ribbon, kiss each half, then cast them into running water, such as a stream or fountain. Bury the remaining halves of the roses together in the earth, asking Venus to bless your spell.

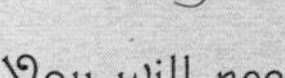

You will need

A red and a white rose

*

A scroll of paper

*

A lock of your hair

*

A short piece of pink ribbon

"Oh Venus, please bring a lover to me, full of warmth and wit and sensuality."

A spell from Eastern Europe to ensure your partner's fidelity.

Nurturing the Seeds of Love

The marigold (*Calendula officinalis*) has long been a symbol of endurance. The word "calendula" comes from the Latin *calends*, which means "the first day of the month." In the Mediterranean, its native climate, this cheerful flower blooms on the first day of every month of the year, giving it an affinity to women and their cycle. In Britain, the marigold used to be called "husband's dial," or "summer's bride," and was often used in wedding garlands and strewn before the bride's cottage door. The marigold has been described as the "comforter of the heart and spirits."

METHOD

First you must secretly dig some earth from your lover's or partner's footprints. It need not be enough to fill the pot completely, but a portion of the soil must come from this source. On a full or waxing moon, when the lunar power is at its height, in late spring or summer, sow your seeds in the pot. As you sow them, hum or sing gently, thinking loving thoughts about your partner. Place your pot by a sunny window, and water and nurture with care. These are special plants and should not be picked, or the strength of the spell will be sapped. In the fall, gather the seeds together and save them to plant the following year in the same way. If you have a garden, choose a special patch for these seeds of love. Marigolds will self-seed for many years to come, symbolizing constancy and endurance as well as beautifying your garden.

You will need

Some soil

*

A small terra-cotta pot

*

A handful of marigold seeds

Fame & Fortune

Seven spells for wealth and success in your career or a business venture, and for special luck in money matters. These spells will not automatically lead you to the pot of gold at the end of the rainbow, but they will enhance your chances of attracting luck and good fortune, and pave your way forward. As with most things in life, it is the effort and sincerity you put into your magic that will reap rich dividends.

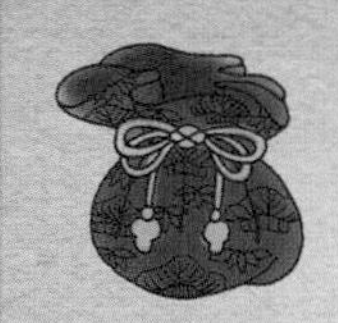

A Mediterranean spell to charge you with the strength to overcome a stressful situation.

Bagging Stress

We all suffer from stress at one time or another, and in a workplace it is often difficult to reverse the situation. This spell can be taken to your workplace or used in other stressful situations, with minimum disturbance. For healing and magic, the earth or Mother Earth, from whence all things spring, is unsurpassed. Add a little borage, the flower of courage, and some of your own essence, and even the most difficult of predicaments can be overcome.

METHOD

Make a small bag. It can be very plain and simple, but it is important that you stitch it together yourself by hand, so that you are putting your self-essence into it. The bag needs to be large enough for you to get both hands inside, with a drawstring to secure it. As a special touch, embroider your initials on it in your favorite color. On a bright, sunny day, collect a few handfuls of dry earth and some borage flowers. Feel the sun's rays warming your body and the flowers and soil in your hands, and store the memory carefully. Dry the borage flowers, then place them with the earth in your bag. Pull the drawstring to secure them. Keep the bag in an accessible place. When things are going badly or you need a pick-me-up, it will only take a few moments to place your hands in the bag, touch the dried borage flowers, reflect on your stored memories, and let Mother Earth work her magic.

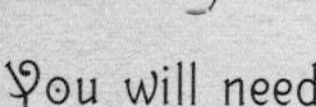

You will need

A handmade cloth bag

*

Some dry earth

*

A small bunch of borage flowers

A Scottish charm for those special occasions when you require luck with money.

Shoon Lore

In many parts of the world, "shoon"—an old Scottish word for shoes—have special significance, partly because they are seen as a symbol of authority. The father of an Anglo-Saxon bride would give one of his daughter's shoes to her new husband, who would then touch her on the head with it, to symbolize the passing of authority over her from her father to her husband. From as far back as the ancient Hebrews, people have associated shoes with the soul. Shoes were also thrown after boats to convey luck. For this good-luck charm to work, the shoes must always be old.

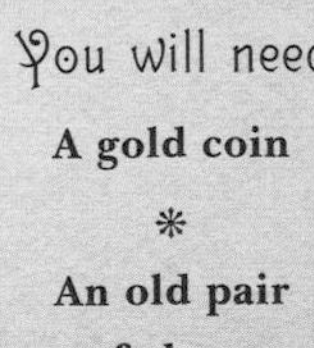

You will need

A gold coin

An old pair of shoes

METHOD

On a Monday morning, charge the gold coin with the power of the sun's rays by holding it up in front of you and saying:

"What I see, may it increase, so I may have financial peace."

Place the gold coin in the left shoe, then put both shoes on. Walk clockwise in a circle three times, then remove the shoes and place them in a T shape where they will not be disturbed. Do exactly the same for three consecutive days. On the third day, transfer the coin to your most regularly worn shoes. Tape the coin inside your shoe and wear it there as often as possible. Do not spend this coin and it will bring you luck.

A Native American spell to bring clarity to a special problem.

Sweating It Out

To Native Americans, the body is a manifestation of the spirit, and to solve a problem you have to be in harmony with your spirit. Although the "sweat lodge" is associated with Native Americans, the ancient Celts, Russians, Japanese, and other European nations had their own sweat houses or baths. Sweating helps to remove toxins from the body, bringing both physical and spiritual balance.

METHOD

Make a miniature sweat lodge—around 10 in. (25 cm) high—from the willow twigs and string by bending and tying the twigs to form a dome shape. Drape the cloth over it, leaving a small gap to represent the door. The sweat lodge is your link to the spirit world. Place seven stones and a sage leaf inside and say:

"Mitakuye oyasin."
(We are all related.)

You will need

3 willow twigs

*

Natural-fiber string and cloth

*

8 small stones

*

2 sage leaves

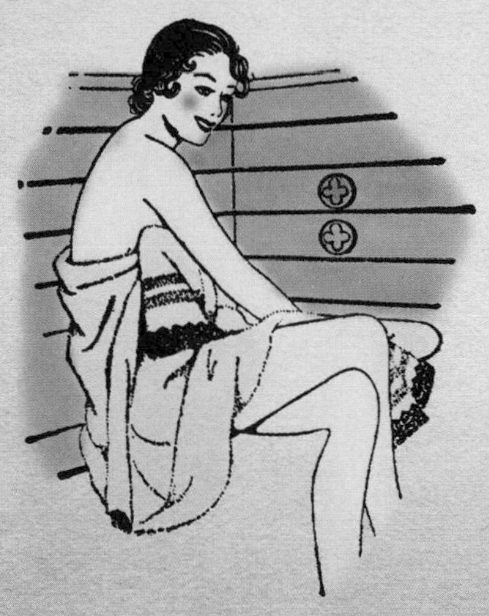

This acknowledges your place in the Circle of Life. Take the remaining stone and sage leaf with you to a local sauna. Hold them in your hands, close your eyes, and think about "mitakuye oyasin." As your body cleanses itself, clarity will return. Place the stone and sage leaf with the others when you return home, and within 24 hours you will have the answer to your problem.

An annual English ritual to pave the way for a good career.

Career Career

Although the oak and acorn are linked closely to the British Isles, the oak tree grows all over Europe. The ancient Druids planted sacred oak groves as guardians, and marriages took place under isolated oaks that also marked the boundaries of a district. In England, some still stand to this day. The native people of California revered the oak as their "world tree," the acorn symbolizing the cosmic egg, from which all life came, and the tree itself symbolizing the cosmic axis, sacred to the Earth Mother. The acorn represents achievement and great effort; the oak tree represents durability, resolution, and truth. A Thursday with a waxing moon is ideal for starting this spell.

You will need

A green candle

*

A piece of green paper

*

2 acorns

*

A silver coin

METHOD

On a Thursday morning, light the green candle. Close your eyes and imagine the candle's light holding you in a safe cocoon. Write your name on the piece of paper, followed by any ambitions you have for your career. Extinguish the candle, and keep it to use again later. For the whole of the day, keep the acorns, silver coin, and paper in a pocket or pouch close to you. On returning home from work, light the candle again, and pass the acorns and silver swiftly through its flame. Wrap the acorns and silver coin in the paper and bury them in your garden, or another favorite spot. Repeat this spell at yearly intervals for continuing career success.

DUE TO THE VASTNESS OF AFRICA, NO UNIFIED CONCEPT OF MAGIC EVER DEVELOPED THAT ENCOMPASSED THE BELIEFS OF THE WHOLE CONTINENT. THE ABUNDANCE OF ANIMAL LIFE DID, HOWEVER, LEAD TO A COMMON BELIEF IN ANIMAL GODS AND SPIRITS.

Ritual ox mask

AFRICAN MAGIC

Symbolic tree

NORTHERN AFRICA

Less than 1,000 years ago, the Sahara Desert was a fertile pasture land. Rock paintings at Tassili n'Ajjer show verdant grasslands, teaming game, and rivers running with fish. In the Sahara and Sahel regions, the universe was thought of as a "cosmic tree." People planted symbolic trees around oases to represent the

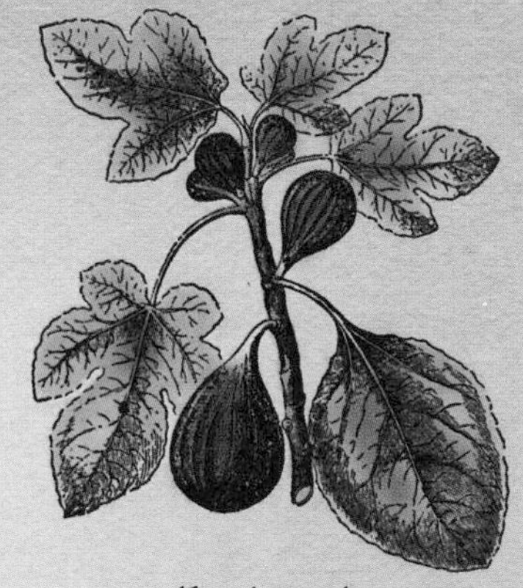

Fig branch

tiers of the universe: a vine for the above world, a grenadine tree for the earth, and a fig tree for the world below. The Yoruba carried out divination using palm nuts. The ceremony was called the "Ifa oracle," and the diviner was always male.

Dance and masks played a huge part in magic and myth, and encapsulated the story of mankind. The Dogon fashioned their masks in caves, away from the prying eyes of the noninitiates. The masks were used in initiation and funeral rites, and for warding off bad spirits. Expulsion rituals in Togo involved cleaning the whole village. All the evils collected were bundled into leaves and creepers, which were hung on poles outside the village. The next morning the women swept their hearths, and the sweepings were taken to a mountain, where they were ceremoniously thrown away.

Ifa divination wand and bowl

Fetish tree

CENTRAL AFRICA

This equatorial forest region is the great mythical Africa, littered with secret societies, sorcerers, healers, and tree spirits. The old Nsoro secret society wore black masks with protruding eyes, played musical instruments, and had their own insignia. The chief of the Teke was believed to be surrounded by a sacred aura that allowed him to see into the next world. His mysterious power was reinforced by the decoration of his face and garments and the possession of magical objects. Leopard teeth were used for his necklace, conferring the animal's strength to him, and cowrie shells were worn in a band around his head, representing connection with spiritual forces.

Komo soothsayers wore oval masks during nighttime divination sessions, and decorated themselves with feathers, bark belts, ivory bracelets, and bells. Protection amulets, made of natural materials such as nutshells and wood, were carried in leather pouches, as in most other African regions.

Cowrie shells

SOUTHERN AFRICA

Cosmic serpent

As in other parts of Africa, most of the rituals that took place here were collective and for the benefit of the community. To bring rain, the Zulu would kill a "heaven bird" and throw it into a pool, so that rain would fall in sympathy. Likewise, the women buried their children up to their necks in the earth, and howled in a pitiful voice, hoping the sky would soften and rain in pity. The great serpent was seen as one of the prime forces of creation, with its head in the sky and its tail in the waters of the earth, linking the two together. The mythology of the cosmic serpent was common to all African regions.

Witch doctors were both medical and spiritual healers. The Caffres used goats to transfer illness from villagers. The goat was daubed with the blood of the sick person and set loose away from habitation. In some places the animal was sacrificed, hence the term "scapegoat." The casting and interpreting of bones is an ancient form of divination. Each bone had a positive side, which was decorated, and a negative side, which was left plain. The bones came from different animals, and were chosen for the qualities displayed by those animals.

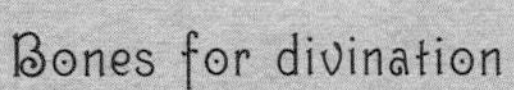

Bones for divination

A series of rites from Native America to aid successful meetings and dispel grudges.

Burying the Hatchet

If you have a difficult meeting coming up, or you need to put problems with your work colleagues behind you, this ritual will help. It will free your mind of irrelevant grudges, and enable you to remain calm for any ordeal ahead. In Native American meetings, or councils, the members sat in a circle to show that, like the spokes of a wheel, every member's input was of equal value. At the start of a council, prayers were spoken and the sacred peace pipe shared. The aim of the council was to put the whole tribe back in balance rather than apportion guilt: no one should judge another person without "walking in their moccasins."

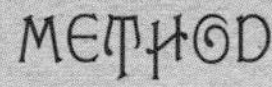

METHOD

Find a symbol of your work, for example, a business card, or of the grudge. If you cannot find a suitable symbol, write a description of your work or the grudge on a small piece of paper. A short while before you go to the meeting, wipe your face and hands with the sage; it is a powerful purifier. At the same time, close your eyes, think about the meeting or grudge, and let go of any preconceived ideas or worries you may have. Put the symbol of your work or grudge, one feather, and the sage leaves together, and bind them with string. Do this with a positive frame of mind, then bury the bundle in the ground, leaving the past behind. Put the remaining feather into a pocket or bag and take it into the meeting with you. Touch it whenever you need to restore your balance, or talk, at the meeting.

You will need

A symbol of your work or grudge, or a pen and paper

*

Some sage leaves

*

2 feathers

*

Some string

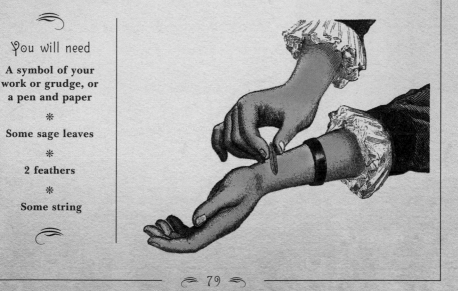

A Celtic spell to improve your success in business over the coming year.

Work Blessing

This spell originates from Ireland and is traditionally performed in February at Imbolc, one of the eight festivals in the Celtic calendar. Birgit, the goddess of creativity, is transformed from her winter appearance of the withered hag into a radiant spring bride, symbolizing new life. Originally, this spell would have been performed near to the hearth, the center of the home, and would have included the whole family, with the women and children fashioning the garland of ivy and the men providing the token offering. If you have no hearth, you can use red candles placed in a small circle.

You will need

Tendrils of ivy leaves

*

Some ribbons

*

A symbol of your work and a token offering

*

Milk and honey

METHOD

Gather the ivy and carefully fashion it into a garland, taking the shape of a St. Bridget's knot. Lay the garland by the hearth or candles, in the circle of light. With love and care, decorate the whole garland with the ribbons, which should be in all your favorite colors. Place the symbol of your work, for example, a business card, in the center of the knot, then place a token offering next to it. The token could be a flower or a coin, for example. Mix a spoon of honey into a glass of warm milk, take a drink, and ask for help with your work for the coming year.

An old English spell to bring luck and success in a business venture.

Apple & Sea

In almost every country it grows, the apple tree has been revered and thought magical. In England, King Arthur recovered from his wounds in the Vale of Avalon, the Apple Vale. In Ireland, apple trees could not be bought with money, but only by bartering another living thing for them, as they were considered too sacred to be tarnished by money. Start this spell at the beginning of a business venture, and continue it for 28 days, a lunar month cycle.

METHOD

At the start of your business, obtain some apple logs or a few twigs. Be sure to touch the tree and ask for its blessing before taking the wood. Soak the apple wood in sea water or brine for 28 days, then dry the wood and burn it on a bonfire or hearth—the smells are a delight! Although wood is best, if you have been unable to obtain any, dry some apple slices, place them around an oil burner, and vaporize some of your favorite essential oil. As the wood or oil burns, repeat three times:

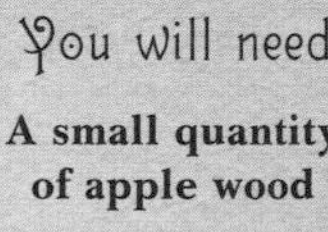

You will need

A small quantity of apple wood

*

Sea water or brine

"May luck continue
in my hand,
and blossom like
an apple bough."

Your business will gradually grow and become successful. Do not worry if you have only been able to burn oil or a very small quantity of wood; this will not affect the quantity of luck.

Labor of Love

Seven spells for family harmony and fertility. At times, a well-balanced home and family life are difficult to achieve. This selection of spells will help you to improve the aura of your home; you will find that other aspects of family life will then automatically fall into place. A happy, relaxed home, free from negative spirits, is a fertile home for mind and body. Even the most daunting of relations and the most fractious of children can be dealt with effectively with a little bit of magic.

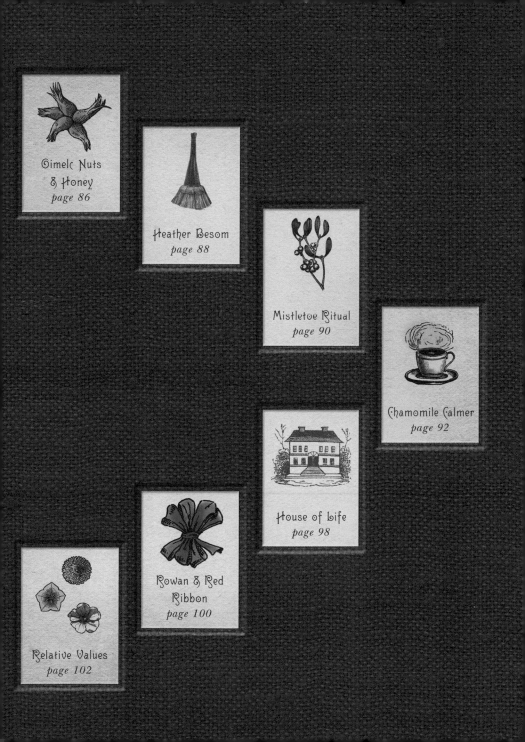

Celtic wisdom to aid conception.

Oimelc Nuts & Honey

Oimelc means "ewe's milk," and is the Celtic name for the early part of February, when the new lambs are born. It has always been a great time of rejoicing; the birth of the new lambs heralds a renewal of life after the cold winter months, with the first green buds of spring appearing and fresh milk to drink. Today, ewe's milk is usually thought of as an unusual health food; in the past, it was an essential part of the staple diet, and easier to digest than cow's milk.

METHOD

From the time you decide you wish to become pregnant, include ewe's-milk yogurt, hazelnuts, and honey in your diet, on a daily basis. At the same time, spend at least 10 minutes each day outdoors, whatever the weather, rain or shine. You can do this with your partner, or alone if you prefer. It should be a silent time when you become as one with your body, letting it absorb the natural rhythms of cosmic energy. Even if you live in the center of a city, search with your senses for all the little nuances of Mother Nature. Feel the rain as it falls; don't hide from it, welcome it. Watch the light dance in its droplets. Listen for birdsong, close your eyes, and let your ears find the source. Open your eyes again, and take all the things around you into your heart. Nurture them within you, and let them grow to give you a deeper contentment and understanding of your inner self and the natural wonders that surround you.

You will need

Pasteurized ewe's-milk yogurt

*

Crushed hazelnuts

*

Honey

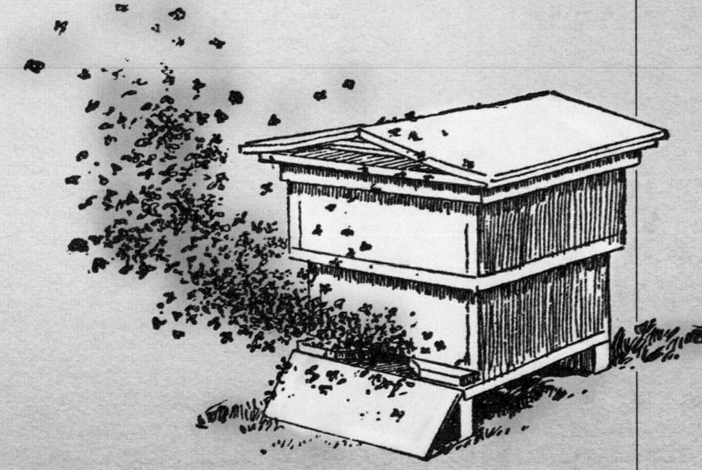

An old English ritual to chase negative spirits from your home.

Heather Besom

There are many traditions linked to the besom, or broom, not least its association with witches. In medieval England, besoms were regarded as essentially feminine tools, and if a woman wished to show she was not at home, she set a broom outside her door. Made from birch, heather, or broom twigs, they were used for gypsy marriages. Known as "broomstick weddings," the ceremony involved the couple jumping back and forth over the broom, holding hands all the while, before a rush ring was placed on the girl's finger. Besoms are still available commercially, but any broom will do if you have difficulty finding a besom.

You will need

A besom or other broom

*

An incense stick

METHOD

Perform this spell on a waning moon. Starting at the highest room in your home, sweep backward through each doorway, symbolically chasing out all bad feelings. At the threshold to your home, sweep backward with a vengeance, then hold the besom aloft and shake it three times into the wind, turning in a counterclockwise direction and saying:

"Spirits fly with the wind; be banished from my way."

Finish the spell by lighting the incense stick in the center of your home to sweeten the atmosphere.

A Druidic ritual to promote fertility.

Mistletoe Ritual

This is a symbolic ritual, designed to put you at ease with the forces of nature and thus aid conception. Mistletoe, or "all-heal," was a sacred plant to the Druids. It was a symbol of immortality and fertility, and was closely linked with magic and medicine. Mistletoe was the soul of the great oak tree, and in the language of flowers, mistletoe means "I surmount all difficulties." Mistletoe grows high in the branches of the trees, in the in-between world, and is golden and green when its host is bare of foliage.

You will need

A green cloth and small table

*

Some sprigs of mistletoe

*

3 green candles

*

A moonstone

METHOD

At the start of the new moon, make a simple fertility altar by draping a green cloth over a small table or shelf. Adorn the altar with the mistletoe and green candles. You can add any other green plants, flowers, or natural elements that have a special significance for you. If you have a personal charm, place this on the altar as well to give added strength to your magic. Each day, stand by the altar and ask the moon goddess to bless you with the powers of creation. At the same time, gently massage your abdomen with the moonstone, and carry the moonstone with you at all times.

Moonstones come in a variety of different shades; a white or yellow stone is the best to use in conjunction with the full moon. On the first full moon after you began the ritual, take a single mistletoe berry from your altar and place it in the forked branch of a tree. Continue to do this as each full moon arrives.

An Anglo-Saxon spell to appease argumentative children.

Chamomile Calmer

In Europe, in the Middle Ages, chamomile was hung over babies' cots to protect them. To the Anglo-Saxons, it was one of the nine sacred herbs, and used as a calmative. In the language of flowers, chamomile is called the "flower of equilibrium." There are times when nothing can seem to stop children from fighting, so exercise this spell with your fractious children when you need a little peace and quiet.

METHOD

With your help, get your children to make a chamomile infusion. Add 1¼ oz. (30 g) of dried chamomile flowers or 2¾ oz. (75 g) of fresh flowers to 17 fl. oz. (500 ml) of boiling water, in a teapot, and leave to infuse for around 10 minutes. Using a strainer, pour yourself a cup to drink, and then strain the rest into a bowl and leave to cool. While it is cooling, get the children to fill the pot with soil, and plant a chamomile each. Teach them this rhyme to chant as they work:

You will need

Chamomile infusion

*

A bowl

*

A large plant pot and some soil

*

Chamomile plants or cuttings

"Show us the charm of flowers, sing us the spell of peace."

When they have finished, let them wash their hands in the warm infusion, together, mingling their essences, then water the plants with it. Tell your children they may make a wish as they water the plants, if they agree to be friends.

Druid priest

In most of Europe, witchcraft was actually the remains of local pagan religions. These religions survived for at least 1,000 years after the introduction of Christianity.

European Magic

The Art of the Wise

The word "witchcraft" means, simply, "the art of the wise." Since the 15th century, the word has been solely applied to those practicing magic, whether male or female. Witchcraft is still practiced in Europe. In France, *esbats*, weekly meetings of witches, still take place, and in Italy, in spite of the Catholic Church, *la vecchia religione* has many followers.

In the 16th and 17th centuries, the huge number of witches sentenced to torture and death shows how widespread witchcraft was, and the sincere belief everyone had in it. The persecution of witches spread rapidly throughout Europe, and thousands of innocent people were killed. In England, 200 witches were executed on evidence given by a single man, Matthew Hopkins, the "witchfinder."

Witch persecutions

Many of these people merely celebrated the pagan feast days and natural festivals of the seasons. In fact, the Christian church also held festivals on these days, but they had become Saints Days, to dissociate the celebrations from their pagan origins. Fertility rites for crops and animal herds attracted special attention from the Christian witch hunters, so the poorest people living close to nature, who used herbs and words to heal, and who were in many cases totally unaware that they were witches, suffered most. Ironically, even the most Christian of Christian symbols, the cross, dates back to pagan times, thousands of years before Christ. The cross is a cosmic symbol, a tree of life, connecting heaven and earth; the vertical arm represents spirituality and the horizontal arm the earthly dimension. A cross was often placed inside a circle, which represented the sun and eternity; together they symbolized the earth and the revolution of the four seasons. This symbol was used for luck and protection in many forms of natural magic.

Celtic cross

ANIMALS AND DIVINATION

The god of the witch cult was always called the devil. "Devil" literally means "little god"; when a new religion surfaces, the god of the old religion often becomes the devil of the new one. The devil was believed to be incarnate in a human being or animal. The earliest example of the devil appearing in human and animal guise is recorded on the walls of a cave in Ariège, in southern France; it shows a man dressed in a stag's skin and wearing antlers. In Germany and France, the goat disguise was common, and probably derived from the god Cernunnos.

Horned devil

Cernunnos

Witch's familiar

The use of familiars for divining was widespread throughout Europe. The leader of a coven of witches would dictate which animal each witch would use as his or her familiar. In France, the familiar was always a toad, which was consulted before any new venture was started. To this day, fire festivals are held on Midsummer's Eve in many parts of Europe, during which cattle are driven through the fires for protection. Couples jump over the flames, throw mugwort and vervain into the fire, and say: "May all my ill-luck depart and be burned up with these." A lighted stick is then taken to rekindle the home fire.

Transference magic was also practiced in Europe, in the belief that an affliction could be transferred from a person to an animal or object. In Wales, an illness was commonly transferred to a chicken, and in Italy, a fever was cured by tying it to a tree.

Vervain

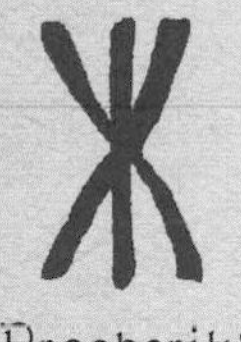
Prosperity

Fertility

RUNIC TRADITIONS

In the Norse tradition, runes were, and still are, used for divination. The runic system used today probably originated in the 3rd century B.C. Each runic symbol represents a letter of the alphabet, but also has a more magical meaning, such as fertility or prosperity. Runic divination involves casting or throwing stones bearing runic symbols, and interpreting them.

Luck

Fidelity

An Egyptian spell to rid the home of bad spirits.

House of Life

The Egyptians trusted implicitly in the power of magic. Their hieroglyphics tell us that: "The word creates all things: everything that we love and hate, the totality of being. Nothing IS before it has been uttered in a clear voice." You can perform this spell on your own or with other members of your family.

You will need

Essential oil and salt

*

Rosemary, sage, and olives

*

A bowl of spring water

*

A long piece of white ribbon

METHOD

Each person taking part should first cleanse themselves by taking a bath containing 7 drops of their favorite oil and a teaspoonful of salt, the emblem of eternity and immortal life. Divide the rosemary, sage, and olives (these are substitutes for olive flowers, the flowers of peace) into four portions, and place a portion in each corner of your home. Quietly put the spring water in a bowl, and with your fingertips, sprinkle some in all the rooms of your home. All those performing the spell should stand in a circle around the remaining spring water. Pass the ribbon in a circle around everybody, turn clockwise, and chant:

"You who enter, do not enter with ill feeling. I have uttered these words over the sacred herbs, placed in all corners of our home, and I have sprinkled each room with sacred water. May it not be haunted by any spirit."

A Druidic charm to bless and protect your home.

Rowan & Red Ribbon

The rowan tree's name is thought to have come from the Norse word *runa*, meaning "a charm." The rowan is the tree of protection, and for hundreds of years its wood has been cut to use as amulets. Rowans are often found near ancient stone circles, and the Druids used both the wood and berries in magical rites. In Scotland, many old houses have chimney lintels made of rowan wood, and on May's Eve, rowan berries were fastened to cows' tails to protect them from evil spirits, abroad on that magical night.

METHOD

Gather two or three rowan twigs. They must be approximately the correct length—around 10 in. (25 cm)—as you must not cut them with a knife. Before taking the twigs, pour a libation of ale at the foot of the tree, to ask for its blessing. Bind the twigs into a cross shape with the red ribbon. Place this talisman to your forehead, to your heart, and then kiss it. Carry it through all the rooms of your home, circling each one with the talisman in your outstretched hand. Walk backward through your front door, and secure the rowan above the door.

You will need

Rowan twigs

*

A bottle of ale

*

A short piece of red ribbon

For continued protection, this ritual should be repeated four times a year, on "quarter days"—March 25th, June 24th, September 29th, and December 25th. To fully appreciate its beauty and efficacy, plant a rowan tree near your home or in a large pot placed to catch the morning sun.

A lunar spell from the East to help you deal with tricky relations.

Relative Values

If for no apparent reason your relationship with your relatives is strained, a magical approach may ease the situation. Before you perform this spell, analyze the reasons for the rift. It is important for you to be as positive as possible, and to avoid areas of conflict, to stabilize the relationship. Perform this spell on a waning moon, to help you drive out the negative feelings.

You will need

Some flowers

*

An incense stick

*

A golden candle

*

A dish of rose water

METHOD

Invite your relations on the evening of a waning moon. Before they arrive, collect the ingredients, which represent the four elements, and place them in the north, south, east, and west of the room where you will be entertaining, as follows:

Flowers, representing earth, in the north;
an incense stick, representing air, in the east;
a golden candle, representing fire, in the south;
some rose water, representing water, in the west.

This will create a magical balance to help proceedings run smoothly. Make an effort to provide plentiful refreshments for your guests, to demonstrate your positive attitude. Light the candle and the incense stick shortly before your guests arrive, and repeat the spell at appropriate intervals.

High Days & Holidays

Seven spells to enhance your enjoyment of holidays and festival days, and to wish you good speed on any journeys undertaken. A strong tradition of celebrating ancient festivals remains with us. Calendars may now show different holiday names, such as Easter and Christmas, but many of them echo customs and rituals that date back to pre-Christian times, with more than a hint of magic in their long histories.

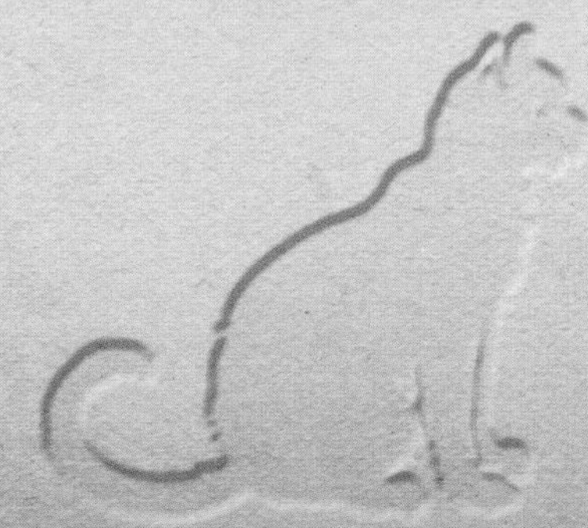

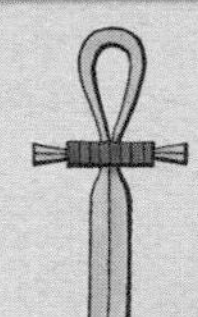

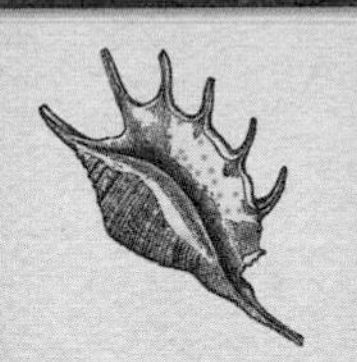

A spell to keep your journeys smooth and free from mishap.

Ginger Rite

Ginger has an honorable history. It was praised by Confucius, and in the Koran, the menu served in Paradise included ginger. It will relieve nausea during pregnancy, and can be chewed raw or in crystallized form to prevent travel sickness. Thursday is a good day to perform this rite, as it is named after Thor, the god of thunder and protection. In Norway, many people named their children Thor, to place them under the god's protection.

You will need

A root of ginger

*

3 yellow ribbons

*

A small wooden box

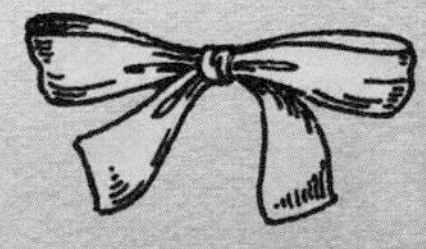

METHOD

When obtaining the ginger, try to secure a root with human form. This is not as difficult as it sounds—gingerroot comes in the most amazing forms. If this is not possible, carefully fashion a body shape with a little knife. Decorate the figure with yellow ribbons tied in three separate places, perhaps the wrists and waist, but not around the neck. As you tie each ribbon, kiss the knot and wish for positive luck in future outings, chanting:

"In all the journeys of my life, protect and keep me safe from strife."

Place the figure in the wooden box, seal the lid, and keep it in a safe, dry place. Make contact with the figure before each major journey, and repeat the rite completely every six months.

A Native American ritual to achieve harmony with your environment.

A Knowing of the Whole

In the past, a Native American traveler entering a strange land would have performed this spell in a place where the elements—earth, air, fire, and water—combine, in order to become part of that spiritual environment. To achieve a state of harmony, the unwritten wisdom of the ages must be absorbed. Today's schedules and environmental factors do not always make this possible, but substitutes can help achieve the same end.

You will need

A yellow candle

*

A flower

*

A bowl of spring water

*

An incense stick

METHOD

Wherever you are in the world, on your arrival, find a private place. Light the candle, for fire, and place it in the south of the room; place the flower, for earth, in the north; the spring water in the west; and the incense stick, for air, in the east. Lie down in the center of your symbols, close your eyes, and use your imagination to see a door in front of you. Go through the door to a luxuriant green paradise, with ladders of sunlight leading upward, and paint a tapestry of colors in your mind as the breeze gently stirs in the leaves. Your eyelids are as heavy as velvet, and a path beckons to you. Follow it, and come to a clearing. In the clearing, sit and thank Mother Earth for her beauty as the sunlight enfolds you in love and peace. Slowly the light fades and you begin your journey back, taking with you a blessing. Open your eyes and stretch, then write down your experience and allow it to grow inside you.

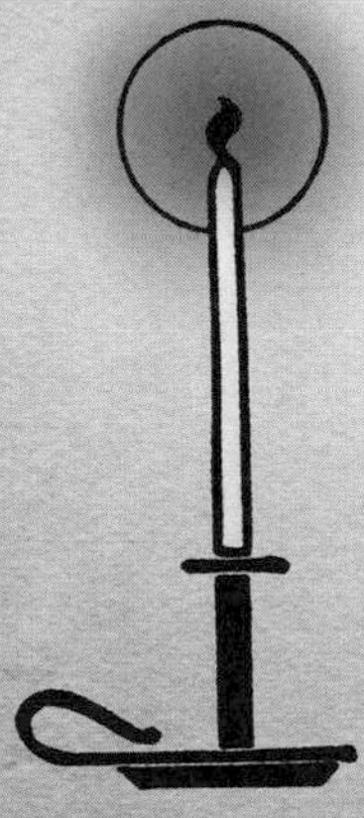

An Egyptian amulet to ward off danger and evil spirits.

Traveler's Amulet

The tradition of wearing or carrying an amulet for protection, particularly when traveling away from home, was practiced by all the ancient civilizations. Specially commissioned and consecrated metals formed many amulets. Birthstones and precious stones, as in a monarch's crown jewels, had special significance and were chosen for their virtues. One of the most ancient amulets is the Egyptian ankh cross, which symbolizes immortality and the power to travel onward. It represents both the male and the female, and is also known as "the key of life."

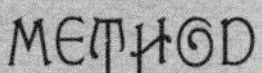

METHOD

The hazel twigs need to be full of sap, so that they will bend without splitting. Fashion them into the shape of an ankh. Bind the twigs together with a strip of silk in your favorite color, or perhaps choose the color associated with your birth sign. Make this charm small, as you need to keep it close to you at all times. As an alternative, commission a blacksmith or jeweler to make the amulet for you. Whichever option you choose, before you wear it, place it to your forehead, then hold it under a full moon to charge it with the moon's rays for added protection.

You will need

2 or 3 slender hazel twigs

*

A strip of colored silk

A May Day spell to incite the luck of the gods for love and good feelings.

May Wish

Celebrating the merry month of May, when spring is in its full glory, is widespread across Europe. May takes its name from Maia Majestas, the goddess of spring. The erection of a sacred tree or maypole echoed ancient tree worship; in Scandinavia, the birch tree was favored. On May's Eve, young couples would leap between the celebration fires before spending the night in the woods, to ensure fertility. The blooming of the hawthorn marked the transition from winter to summer, and May 1st was the only day when hawthorn could be taken into the home, in honor of the spring goddess; this sacred tree could only be cut for such an important purpose.

METHOD

On May 1st, find a hawthorn tree and take a few sprays. Pour a little milk at the base of the tree to thank the spirits. Sit with the tree for as long as you can, holding the hawthorn sprays in your hands, and become as one with the life surrounding you. On your return home, light the candle and burn the oils, sprinkling a few hawthorn leaves on them. Carry the burner through your home or around the outside; concentrate on bringing down the energy from the sun and returning it again in the never-ending Circle of Life. Hang the hawthorn spray over your door, invoking love and good feelings to remain with you.

You will need

A few sprigs of hawthorn

*

A little milk

*

A white candle

*

Juniper and frankincense oils, and an oil burner

DIVERSE FORMS OF MAGIC HAVE BEEN PRACTICED THROUGHOUT THE FAR EAST FOR MANY CENTURIES. THE USE OF OILS, HERBS, SPICES, AND SYMBOLS IN CONNECTION WITH THE MYRIAD DEITIES OF THESE REGIONS WAS COMMON PRACTICE. USUALLY, MAGIC WAS PERFORMED TO ENABLE THE PRACTITIONER TO REACH A HIGHER MENTAL STATE OF EXISTENCE.

MAGIC of the FAR EAST

Brahma, Vishnu, and Shiva

INDIA

Indian myth, magic, and religion have developed over the past 3,500 years by gradually incorporating new beliefs into existing ones. As a result, India has a more complex and diverse nature of beliefs than anywhere else in the world. It has even been said of India that: "There are more gods than men."

Indra

A vast collection of Indian myths is recorded in the *Rig Veda*, an ancient book of hymns. In the Vedic hymns, Indra is king of the Hindu gods, with authority over the sky. He carries a thunderbolt in his right hand, which he uses to do battle with the drought demons to bring rain to the land every year before the rainy season. Before each annual battle, he consumes a magical drink called *soma*, the elixir of immortality. His first great victory was to slay Vintra, the serpent who lay coiled around the world mountain.

Other gods in the hymns include Agni, the god of fire, who symbolizes the vital spark in all life. He acts as an intermediary between the gods and man, and is still revered today, in domestic and ritual fire feasts. Brahma is the creator god, and one of the Hindu triad, together with Vishnu, the protector of the world, and Shiva, the destroyer. The aim of Indian mystics is to escape from the cyclic pattern of birth, death, and rebirth, and enter a higher state of consciousness or being.

Agni

CHINA AND JAPAN

China is the oldest civilization in the world. The material structure of the Chinese world is made up of five elements; five is a magical number to the Chinese. These elements—wood, fire, soil, metal, and water—equate to the five seasons, which include a mystical "center"; the cardinal directions, also including a "center"; and to five planets. The Chinese New Year and other festivals are linked to the lunar calendar. Fireworks and a cacophony of drums and cymbals are used to drive off evil at the turn of the year. Chinese divination is based on the "yin" and "yang." Yang means sunshine and light, and represents masculinity; yin means shadow or darkness, and represents femininity. Yin and yang are seen as mutually dependent, and represent the natural laws of the universe.

Yin/yang symbol

In Japan, Shinto is the oldest belief system. It centers on the worship of *kami*, gods that inhabit all nature and human beings. Shrine festivals are held where an image of the local kami is carried aloft by young men and women, to

The kami Amaterasu

purify the neighborhood and the bearers. Amaterasu, the sun goddess, is one of the greatest deities in Japan. Her main shrine at Ise has been rebuilt in its same form of cypress and thatch since the 7th century.

SOUTHEAST ASIA

Much of the cultural tradition of Southeast Asia has been influenced by China and India; only a few places clung to their own ways. In Bali, rituals were performed at crossroads to expel devils. A horn was blown to summon the devils, then men, carrying torches and wearing fearsome ceremonial masks, chased the devils away. Silence then prevailed for 24 hours, so that the devils would think the island was uninhabited.

The Balinese demon Rahu

In Borneo, a fruit tree was planted for every newborn baby, in the belief that the fate of the child was tied to the growth of the tree. The souls of ancestors were thought to live in trees in the Philippines, and the islanders bowed to the trees as they passed them. In Java, if a feast was to be held in the rainy season, the witch doctor was asked to "prop up the clouds."

Javanese mask

A Celtic rite to let go of the troubles and sadness of the past year.

Samhain Rite

This spell should be performed on November 1st. The fire feast of Samhain was held in this month to celebrate the beginning of the Celtic new year. November is the in-between time, when the veil between the past and present, the living and the dead, is thin. As a month of endings and beginnings, when the seeds of renewal are shed from the mother plant, it is a time to rid yourself of the past and look forward to the future.

You will need

A personal possession

*

A purple candle

*

A small wicker basket

*

A bell

METHOD

The personal possession should embody all that you wish to cast aside, in order that you can start afresh. On the first hour of November 1st, light the purple candle, and place the unwanted possession in the basket. Seal the lid with a little candle wax. Hold the basket, concentrate on the glow of the candle, ring the bell three times, and chant:

"Spirits on this special night,
collect my past and hear my plight,
I mean no harm but do entreat,
a future blossoming and sweet."

Repeat this three times, ringing the bell between the chants. The next morning, take the basket and bury it.

A Norse sea spell to help you heal old wounds and make a fresh start.

White Horses

This spell has its origins in the Norse culture, where diverse traditions grew up around the sea. Perform this spell for help in making a fresh start, whether with a new love, a change of job, or for healing a breach in a relationship. Of all water magic, that which flows from the sea is the most potent. The tides are ruled by the moon, and are at their most magical during the phases of the new and full moons.

Travel to a quiet seashore and carry out this spell on an incoming tide, when the moon is newest.

METHOD

Hold the silver coin, the two shells, and the vervain leaves in your outstretched hand, and ask for the moon's blessing. Drink a toast to the sea and moon, and rest awhile until your mind is clear with your purpose. Throw one shell as far as you can into the waves, chanting your wish as you do so. With the other shell, write your wish and your name in the sand, below the hightide mark. Wrap the shell and silver coin in the vervain leaves, count seven waves coming in, then bury the bundle in the sand in the center of your message. Retire and wait for the incoming tide to receive your wishes. As you wait, chant:

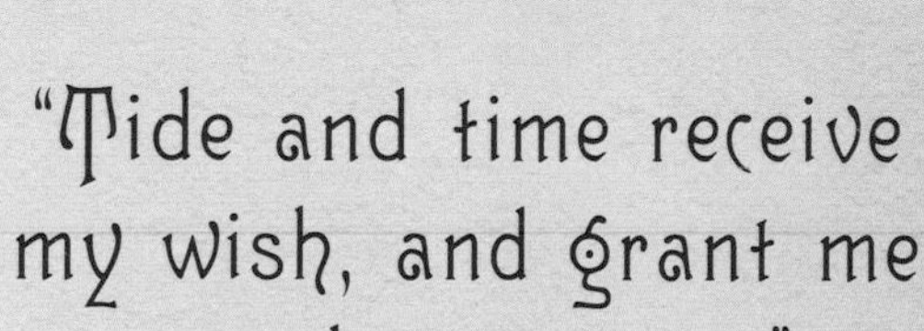

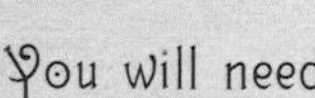

You will need

A silver coin

*

2 shells

*

Fresh or dried vervain leaves

*

A flask of wine

"Tide and time receive my wish, and grant me new beginnings."

A Russian spell to ease your way forward at the darkest time of year.

A Spell for Yuletide

Yul means "wheel," and in earlier times, this was the yoke of the year, the time of turning and going forward. Onions and salt are both purifiers, and will help to ease your way over this period to make new beginnings. In Russia, the birch was used at Christmastime as a symbol of rebirth, and also at Whitsun, when it was dressed in female clothing to welcome the summer in.

You will need

3 white candles

*

2 small onions and some red cord

*

A little salt

*

2 silver birch twigs

METHOD

At the eve of the winter solstice, December 21st, light the candles. While focusing on their light, peel the onions and thread or bind them with red cord, saying:

"Spirits of the past and present,
keep evil sorts at bay;
harmony and joy prevail,
at the turning of the day."

Hang the onions at the front and back doors of your home. If you do not have a back door, use a window instead. On Christmas Eve, take down the onions and sprinkle them with salt. Remove the cord, then burn or bury the onions. Place the silver birch twigs to your forehead, then hang them at your front and back doors with the red cord in place of the onions.

Lucky Charms & Life Savers

Seven spells for luck, an essential ingredient for a charmed life. Four of the spells will help you keep a cheerful outlook and a positive mind, the best recipe for attracting luck. The remaining three spells are printed on sealed pages. These are powerful expelling spells, to remove negative influences, and bring luck and harmony in their place. They should be executed without malice. Think carefully before you open these pages. You may be able to dupe yourself about your motives, but if you are set on causing harm, it will be a fool's errand, and rebound where it began, with you.

A spell for good luck and for the granting of wishes.

Encompassing Luck

Food has long been a symbol of magic. Writing on cakes and other types of food dates back to ancient Greece and goddess worship. Honey cakes were written on, candles lit and blown out, and the wishes on the cakes were eaten to transfer them to the eater. Perform this spell at any time of year on a waxing moon. The red candles are for luck and the green candles for prosperity, but you may wish to substitute other colors more suitable to your specific wish. The seeds hold the promise of regrowth.

METHOD

Alternating the color of the candles, make a large circle with them, aligning them to the eight compass directions: north, northeast, east, southeast, south, southwest, west, and northwest. Put the glass of wine in the center of the circle, and place a dish of seeds or nuts next to it. Keep the pebble in your left hand throughout the spell. It represents the ever-turning Circle of Life and the universe. Light the north candle first, then travel to the center of the circle. Dip a seed or nut into the wine, and making your wish, eat it. Repeat until all the candles are alight, working your way around the circle in a clockwise direction. You may find it helpful to break your wish down into a series of eight steps, and to visualize an individual step as you light each candle. When you have finished, sit in the middle of your glowing circle. Drink the rest of the wine as a toast to the world, and keep the pebble as a lucky charm.

You will need

4 red and 4 green candles

*

A glass of wine

*

Some edible seeds or nuts

*

A round pebble

Chinese sky magic for luck, happiness, and success.

Raising the Wind

Air magic is used in China, where streamers and kites are released skyward bearing messages and pictures. The triad gods of happiness are often depicted. These are Shou-hsing, the god of long life; Fu-hsing, the god of happiness; and Lu-hsing, the god of salaries. Sometimes, the gods are represented symbolically: a bat for happiness, a deer for salaries, and a stork or pine for long life. Dragons, which are divinities of rain and sea, are also popular symbols. Sky or air magic is directed toward personal success, luck, and joy. "Raising the Wind" is an ancient form of sky magic, which can be used to change your luck and convey you toward success.

METHOD

On a windy day, travel to the top of a hill or to an open expanse of beach. Fasten the balloon to the length of string, and as you walk, tie knots in the string. Concentrate on the change or changes you wish to occur when you tie each knot. Imagine the energy rising from your body through the string to the sky, and run with the balloon trailing behind you and tugging to be free. Turn around seven times in a clockwise direction, feeling the power of the wind enter you and raise your spirits. Undo the knots and let the balloon fly away, freeing the spell to bring success and happiness to you.

You will need

A degradable helium-filled balloon

*

A long piece of string

MAGIC RITUALS, LARGELY PERFORMED IN CONJUNCTION WITH NATURE AND FOR THE BENEFIT OF THE WHOLE COMMUNITY, HAVE DEVELOPED IN ALL PARTS OF THE WORLD. BUT THERE IS ALSO A MORE SINISTER SIDE TO THE ART. FROM THE EARLIEST TIMES, PRACTITIONERS REALIZED THE GREAT POWER THAT MAGIC BESTOWED UPON THEM, AND THAT IT COULD BE USED FOR PERSONAL GAIN.

the SINISTER SIDE of MAGIC

Medieval alchemist

ALCHEMISTS AND SORCERERS

Alchemy was a combination of philosophical, scientific, and religious beliefs whose origins are lost in the mists of time. Medieval alchemists reasoned that if nature had the ability to produce a tree from a tiny seed, they could copy this miraculous natural process, and transmute base metal into gold or silver. The "philosopher's stone" was the substance believed to have the power to perform this transmutation. It was also thought to be the power behind the evolution of life. Alchemists used the sun to symbolize gold and the soul, and the moon to symbolize silver and the body. The philosopher's stone was a combination of sulfur, salt, and mercury, the latter often equated to a winged dragon, an ancient symbol of volatile change.

Alchemical symbols for silver, associated with the moon

The fundamental purpose of alchemy was to refresh and restore the earth, but many alchemists strayed from this path. They formed a select society, the master magicians, working in complete secrecy. They became immersed in demonism, in the hope of riches, and in a quest for supernatural powers. They believed that by making magical pacts with the devil and his demon princes, the demons would serve the magician for the rest of his life.

Winged dragon, associated with mercury

However, after death, the sorcerer would in turn become the slave of the demon princes. Consequently, the magician would go to any lengths to prolong his own life, including necromancy and offering live sacrifices. When making a pact with the devil, the magician had to sign a document with his own blood, for it was said: "He controls the soul who controls the blood of another."

Pact signed in blood

THE SIGN OF THE CLOVEN HOOF

The practitioner of such sorcery could not use the benevolent signs and symbols of natural magic, as these would only bring failure. Instead, the symbols had to be inverted or distorted to denote perverted power. The swastika is one example of this. It actually derives from a Sanskrit word meaning "bringer of good luck," and in many cultures it was for centuries a symbol of happiness and good fortune. Now, however, it is an embodiment of all the evils of the world, after a left-handed swastika rather than a right-handed one was used as the insignia of the Nazi party.

Cloven-hoofed demon

The pentagram has been much used in both good and evil magic, but for the latter, it was either inverted, had a break in the star, or had points of different lengths. When altered in this way, it was called the "sign of the cloven hoof."

Pentagram for good magic

Pentagram for evil magic

Double-sided effigy

THE USE OF EFFIGIES

Clay, wax, and wooden dolls have all been used in rites in attempts to harm an enemy. The dolls were bound, stuck with pins or nails, burned, melted, or buried, to cause the demise of the intended victim. Images were sometimes made from a mixture of fat and grain and burned in a place the victim frequented, to capture that person's soul. Some dolls had different-colored sides, one for casting evil spells and one for good spells. Drawing the image of a person in the earth and stabbing it with a pointed stick was thought to transfer an injury to the person being drawn.

The demonism of ancient times was used to attain selfish desires and gain power through any means, with no regard for the harm it could cause. Such magic is a dangerous art and should not be tampered with.

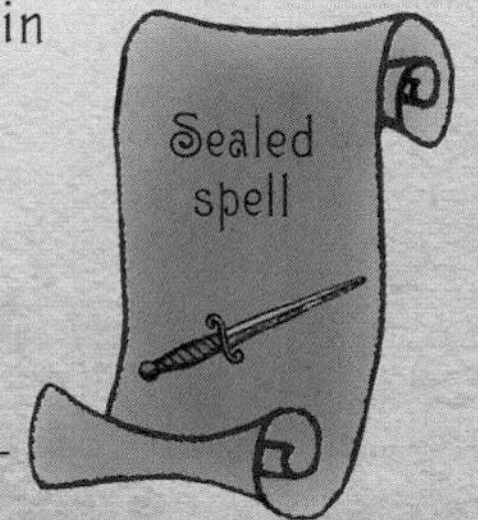

Sealed spell

A spell for continued luck throughout the year and for special days.

Planets & Plants

This spell uses the gifts of nature to bring good luck. It is especially useful for ensuring success when performing other spells, by harnessing the power of Mother Nature to bring luck to all your ventures on a particular day.

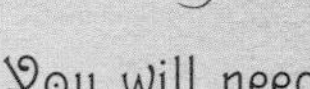

You will need

A large plant pot

*

Some soil

*

A selection of seedlings or cuttings

METHOD

Each day of the week is ruled by a planet, and each of those planets is associated with a particular color. Plant an indoor or outdoor selection of herbs and plants in the color that corresponds to the day on which you require extra luck. The particular plants you choose is personal preference. What is important is to nurture them with love and care, which in return will bring harmony of spirit, body, and mind to you.

The Sun rules Sunday and its color is orange.

The Moon rules Monday and its color is white.

Mars rules Tuesday and its color is red.

Mercury rules Wednesday and its color is yellow.

Jupiter rules Thursday and its color is purple.

Venus rules Friday and its color is blue.

Saturn rules Saturday and its color is green.

Good luck!

A summer spell for luck and the happiness of childhood.

Day's Eye

The name "daisy" comes from "day's eye," as the flower opens at dawn with the sun, and closes at dusk. It is a symbol of luck and innocence because of its association with children. It is also a symbol of survival, as a daisy adapts to almost any growing conditions or landscape, and staunchly survives the lawnmower or hoe. The following charm can be carried out on any sunny day, preferably in a meadow, although any small patch of daisies will do.

You will need

A field of daisies

*

A small, yellow velvet pouch

METHOD

On a beautiful summer's day, take time to sit with a child or children, and make daisy chains. As you work, spin the children a story about the cheerful daisy, and how it is the "day's eye," known throughout the world for its merry face. Talk of medieval knights, who wore a daisy as a token of their lady's love; of how the daisy may be picked or trampled underfoot, but still comes up each year smiling; and about young girls of the past, who slept with a daisy root under their pillows to dream of love. When you have fashioned your own daisy chain, close your eyes, place it to your forehead, and wish for luck. When the children have finished their chains, place them on their heads as chaplets, and then do the same with your own. Join hands and dance in a circle, seven times to the east and seven times to the west, thanking Mother Earth for her blessings. Finally, place your own daisy chain in the pouch, and carry it with you to keep your luck safe.

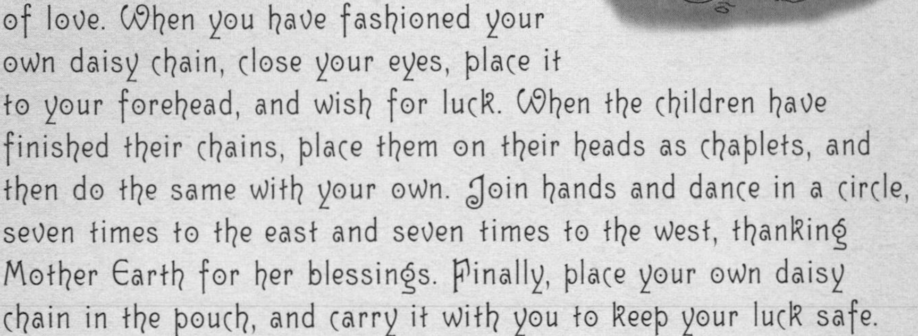

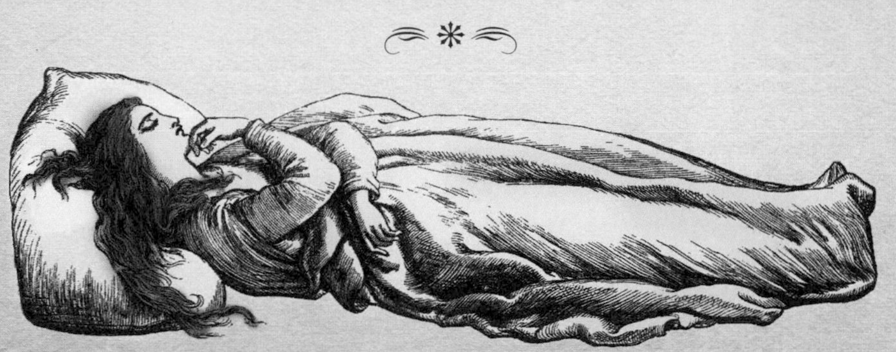

INDEX